OXFORD INTENSIVE ENGLISH COURSES

STUDENT'S BOOK

DAVID BOLTON
CLIVE OXENDEN
LEN PETERSON

Oxford University Press

Oxford University Press
Walton Street, Oxford OX2 6DP

Oxford New York
Athens Auckland Bangkok Bogota Bombay
Buenos Aires Calcutta Cape Town Dar es Salaam
Delhi Florence Hong Kong Istanbul Karachi
Kuala Lumpur Madras Madrid Melbourne
Mexico City Nairobi Paris Singapore
Taipei Tokyo Toronto

and associated companies in
Berlin Ibadan

OXFORD and OXFORD ENGLISH
are trade marks of Oxford University Press

ISBN 0 19 432353 6

Typeset by Pentacor Ltd, High Wycombe, Bucks
Printed in Hong Kong

The authors would like to acknowledge the help and cooperation of
the following schools in the production of this course:

Abon Language School, Bristol; Alos Centro Europeo de Idiomas, Valencia;
IHSP, Bromley; ITS Hastings; King's School, Beckenham; The British
Institute, Valencia

and the following people at Oxford University Press:

Alison Findlay, Coralie Green, Yvonne de Henseler, Jean Hindmarch,
Claire Nicholl, Rosemary Nixon, James Richardson, Greg Sweentnam,
Andy Younger.

Special thanks also go to Paul Power, Gill Hamilton, Fiona Wright
and Simon Taylor.

The publishers would like to thank the following photographic libraries
for their permission to reproduce photographs:

Britain On View, Hutchinson Library, Impact Photos, Rex Features,
Telecom Technology Showcases London.

ILC Hastings; Midland Bank Plc.; Oxford Academy Language School;
Radio Taxis;
Rymans; Salisburys – Handbags Ltd; Samuel H. Plc, Jewellers;
Sylvestr Furniture; Watson A. & Sons Ltd, Menswear.

Illustrations by:

Kate Charlesworth, Dave Cockcroft, Susannah English, Conny Jude,
Maggie Ling, Andrew MacConville, Mohsen John Modaberi, RDH Artists,
Christine Roche, Nich Sharratt, Paul Thomas.

Location and studio photography by:

Cathy Blackie, Rob Judges, Mark Mason.

CONTENTS

UNIT	LESSON 1 GRAMMAR IN ACTION	LESSON 2 ENGLISH IN SITUATIONS	LESSON 3 FUN WITH ENGLISH
1 PAGES 6–11	*to be* possessive adjectives apostrophe 's' genitive	introductions greetings countries and nationalities apologizing saying goodbye	*Further practice in:* pronunciation listening vocabulary reading finding out about the UK
2 PAGES 12–17	demonstratives plural nouns *here/there* definite article	asking and describing where things/places are thanking and responding to thanks	*Further practice in:* pronunciation listening vocabulary reading finding out about the UK
3 PAGES 18–23	*have got* indefinite articles *a/an* – adjective + noun	the alphabet and spelling asking somebody to repeat something using a payphone and making an international phone call	*Further practice in:* pronunciation listening spelling reading finding out about the UK
4 PAGES 24–29	present simple: incl. *do*-construction	telling the time making requests making offers accepting and refusing food	*Further practice in:* pronunciation listening vocabulary reading finding out about the UK
5 PAGES 30–35	present simple: incl. *do*-construction adverbs of frequency	asking for things asking and talking about the cost of things	*Further practice in:* pronunciation listening vocabulary spelling reading finding out about the UK
6 PAGES 36–41	*can/can't*	talking about rules and obligations	*Further practice in:* pronunciation listening vocabulary reading finding out about the UK

UNIT	LESSON 1	LESSON 2	LESSON 3
	GRAMMAR IN ACTION	ENGLISH IN SITUATIONS	FUN WITH ENGLISH
7 PAGES 42–47	present continuous for present time	using the telephone taking messages on the telephone	*Further practice in:* pronunciation listening vocabulary reading finding out about the UK
8 PAGES 48–53	*there is/are* *some/any*	inviting making offers accepting/refusing invitations and offers apologizing and making excuses	*Further practice in:* pronunciation listening vocabulary spelling reading finding out about the UK
9 PAGES 54–59	past simple: regular verbs *was/were*	making arrangements making suggestions making excuses	*Further practice in:* pronunciation listening vocabulary reading finding out about the UK
10 PAGES 60–65	past simple: irregular verbs	buying clothes – talking about sizes and colours	*Further practice in:* pronunciation listening vocabulary reading finding out about the UK
11 PAGES 66–71	comparatives/superlatives	asking permission giving/refusing permission talking about dates	*Further practice in:* pronunciation listening vocabulary reading finding out about the UK
12 PAGES 72–77	future: *going to*	saying goodbye revision of various functions	London picture quiz UK quiz

UNIT ONE

LESSON ONE

First meeting

Dominique is a French boy. He is sixteen. He is in England for the first time. He is on an English language course

I Questions and answers

a Match the questions on the left with the answers on the right.

Example: I – f

1 Is Mr Bond French?
2 Is Dominique on an English language course?
3 Is Mrs Bond rude to Dominique?
4 Are Mr and Mrs Bond English?
5 Is Mrs Bond's first name Sue?
6 Is Miss Fox a student?
7 Are Dominique's bags heavy?
8 Is Dominique's surname Fox?

a) No, they aren't.
b) Yes, it is.
c) Yes, they are.
d) No, it isn't.
e) Yes, he is.
f) No, he isn't.
g) No, she isn't.
h) No, she isn't.

b Work in pairs. Student A asks the same questions. Student B answers them without looking at the answers above. Change roles.

2 You and Dominique

In what ways are you different from Dominique?

a Write sentences like this:

Dominique's French but I'm not. I'm Italian.
Dominique's tall but I'm not. I'm quite short.

b Read out your answers in class.

3 Find out

a What are the questions to get the following information?

	First name	Surname	Age	Nationality	Town	First time in England
Student I						
Student 2						
Student 3						

Examples:
What's your first name?
How old are you?

b Move round the class and ask three students the questions. Fill in the form.

4 Memory game

a The teacher points at a student in the class (student A). That student stands up. Other students in the class say what they can remember about him/her.

Example:
B *His name's Paul.*
C *He's 15.*
D *He's from Menton.*

b The teacher points at another student and the game continues in the same way.

5 What's missing?

I   ..my..

.... our

it   ....

.... his

they   ....

.... her

you   ....

6 Whose is it?

a Each student gives the teacher one thing.

Examples:
a comb, a key, a lipstick, a watch

b The teacher holds up one thing at a time and asks 'Whose is it?'

c Students answer 'It's Mario's' or 'It's Julia's', etc. (You must **not** answer if the thing is yours!)

Grammar summary: page 82

7

1 Introductions

a  Practise this dialogue in pairs.

A *Hello. I'm Sue.*
B *Hello. My name's Dominique.*

b Now practise with the other students in the class. Use your own names.

c Practise the following dialogue in groups of three.
Use your own names. Take it in turn to be A, B and C.

A *(Dominique), this is (Steve).*
B *Hello, (Dominique). Nice to meet you.*
C *Hello, (Steve).*

Note: You may hear older people say 'How do you do?' The answer is 'How do you do?'

2 Greetings

a  Practise this dialogue in pairs.

A <u>Hello.</u> How are you?
B <u>Fine,</u> thanks.

b Now use these words instead of the underlined words.

A	B
(Good) morning	Very well
(Good) afternoon	All right
(Good) evening	Not too bad
Hi	OK

3 Countries and nationalities

Look at the map below.

Per Eklund	Juan and Luis Gomez	Paola Pavoni
Swedish	Spanish	Italian

Hans Bauer	Danielle Ricard and Claire Farge	Karen Olsen
Swiss	French	Danish

a Work in pairs. Ask and answer questions like these about countries.

Examples:
A *Where's Danielle from?*
B *She's from France.*

A *Where are Juan and Luis from?*
B *They're from Spain.*

b Now ask about nationalities in the same way.

Examples:
A *Is Hans Swiss?*
B *Yes, he is.*

A *Is Per Danish?*
B *No, he isn't. He's Swedish.*

A *Are Juan and Luis French?*
B *No, they aren't. They're Spanish.*

C Write sentences about the people on the map.

Examples:
Paola's Italian.
Danielle and Claire are from France.
Hans isn't from Germany. He's from Switzerland.

4 Where am I from?

Form two teams (A and B). Each team prepares a list of cities from different countries.
One student in team A then says, for example: 'I'm from Athens.' The students in team B must then say 'You're Greek.' or 'You're from Greece.' to get a point. Team A gets a point if team B can't answer or if the answer is wrong. One student in team B then says the name of another city, and so on.

5 What's missing?

🖳 Listen and fill in the missing information.

Name	Age	Country	Nationality
Ria Muhren			
Hans Beck			
Estelle Verrier			
Manuel Santos			
Maki Tadeshi			
Miguel Salazar			

6 Saying you're sorry

a 🖳 Practise these conversations in pairs.

A *I'm sorry he's so rude.*
B *That's all right.*

A *I'm sorry I'm late.*
B *That's OK.*

b In two groups, A and B, think of different reasons for saying 'I'm sorry . . .'
One student from group A then apologizes, and a student from group B responds.
One student from team B then apologizes, and a student from team A responds, and so on.

7 Saying goodbye

a 🖳 Practise this conversation in pairs. Take it in turn to be A and B.

A *Bye.*
B *Bye. See you <u>tomorrow</u>.*

b Now use these words instead.

A	B
Goodbye	soon
Bye-bye	on Monday
Cheerio	next week

Summary of English in situations

- introducing yourself and other people
- greeting people
- talking about countries and nationalities
- saying you're sorry
- saying goodbye

1 Sound right

a Find pairs of words which rhyme.

Example:
no – so

what	there
are	too
for	not
my	car
where	your
you	SO
NO	I

b Form two teams. The teacher writes words from the two lists on the blackboard. The teams take it in turn to add words to the lists. The words *must* rhyme but you must *not* write words from the other team's list.

The team with the longest list is the winner.

c Now practise pronouncing the groups of rhyming words on the blackboard.

2 Listen to this

Listen to the following short conversations. Where do they take place? Write the correct number under each picture. Listen to the example first.

a ....

e ....

b ....

c ....

d ....

f ....

3 Work on words

Find the opposites. Match the words on the left with their opposites on the right.

Example:
yes – no

boy	light
YES	polite
first	horrible
good	tall
Mr	evening
here	goodbye
nice	woman
husband	there
rude	wife
hello	last
heavy	bad
short	late
early	NO
man	Mrs
morning	girl

4 Play games in English

Who are you?

a One student at a time thinks of a famous person.

The other students ask him/her questions like this:
Are you alive/dead?
Are you a man/a woman?
Are you English/American? etc.
Are you a politician/film star/pop singer? etc.

The student can only answer 'Yes, I am' or 'No, I'm not'.

b The student who gets the right answer then thinks of another famous person and the rest of the class ask him/her questions.

5 Read and think

Look at these words.

circle   triangle   square   cross   line

Now follow these instructions.

1 Write your first name on the line under the big square.
2 Put a cross in the small circle if you're not English.
3 Put a square in the big circle if you're a student.
4 Write your surname in the big square on the right.
5 Put a small cross on top of the big square if you're a girl.
6 Put a cross in the top triangle if you're fourteen.
7 Put a circle in the bottom triangle if you're in England for the first time.
8 Put a cross in the square on the left if you're on an English language course.
9 Put a small circle under the small square on the right if you're a boy.

6 Now you're here

British money

a Learn the value of these British coins.

b Take out your British money. Work in pairs. Student A puts some money on the desk. Student B says how much there is. Change roles.

UNIT TWO
LESSON ONE

Dominique's room

These bags are heavy!

This is the bathroom in here.

Oh yes.

Um . . . where's the toilet?

Oh, the loo! That's the loo over there.

That's our bedroom . . . and this is your room.

That's the wardrobe there and these drawers are for your clothes.

Oh, it's very nice . . . um . . . and it's quite big.

Right, thanks.

1 Right or wrong?

Tick (√) the correct answer.

		Right	Wrong
1	Dominique's bags are heavy.	✓	☐
2	The bathroom's downstairs.	☐	☐
3	The toilet's in the bathroom.	☐	☐
4	'Loo' is another word for 'toilet'.	☐	☐
5	Dominique's bedroom's quite small.	☐	☐
6	There's a wardrobe in the bathroom.	☐	☐
7	A wardrobe's for books.	☐	☐
8	The drawers are for Dominique's clothes.	☐	☐
9	Dominique's a boy's name and a girl's name.	☐	☐

I'm sorry about all the flowers, and the doll . . . But Dominique is a girl's name.

That's all right, Mrs Bond. I like flowers too.

2 Where are they?

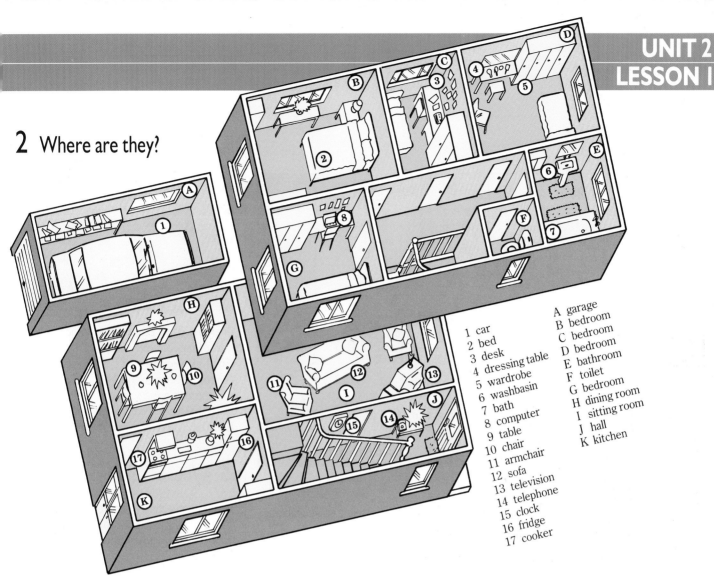

1 car
2 bed
3 desk
4 dressing table
5 wardrobe
6 washbasin
7 bath
8 computer
9 table
10 chair
11 armchair
12 sofa
13 television
14 telephone
15 clock
16 fridge
17 cooker

A garage
B bedroom
C bedroom
D bedroom
E bathroom
F toilet
G bedroom
H dining room
I sitting room
J hall
K kitchen

Work in pairs. Ask and answer questions about the Bonds' house.

Examples:
A *Where's the fridge?*
B *It's in the kitchen.*

A *Where are the armchairs?*
B *They're in the sitting room.*

3 Make changes

Change these sentences from singular to plural.

Example:
This chair's heavy.
These chairs are heavy.

1 That's our bedroom.
2 This drawer's full.
3 This room's a bedroom.
4 That bedroom's big.
5 That's Dominique's bag.
6 This is her book.

4 Your home

a Draw a plan of the house or flat you're living in in Britain, or your house or flat at home, like this:

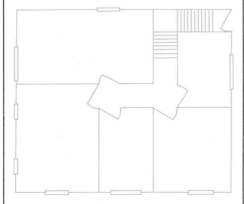

b Work in pairs. Give your plan to another student. Student A points to one room on student B's plan and asks:

A *What's this room?*
B *That's the sitting room.*

C Add some furniture to your plans, like this:

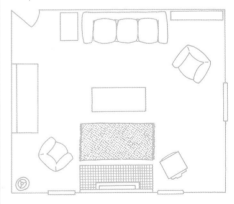

d Ask each other questions like this:

A *What are these?*
B *They're armchairs.*

Grammar summary: page 82

1 Where are they?

Picture A

a Fill in the gaps, using words and phrases from the box below.

Example:
The computer's on the desk.

1 The cassettes are . . . the drawer.
2 The Walkman's . . . the desk.
3 The Amstrad's . . . the Walkman.
4 The posters are . . . the desk.
5 The small table's . . . the window.
6 The clothes are . . . the floor.
7 The stereo's . . . the desk.
8 The stereo's . . . the wardrobe.
9 The lamp's . . . the corner.
10 The records are . . . the stereo.

```
in . . .
on . . .
next to . . .
on the right/left of . . .
above/below . . .
```

b Ask the person next to you about the picture above.

Examples:
Where's the lamp?
Where are the clothes?

2 What's different?

a Work in pairs. Student A looks at the picture in exercise 1 (picture A). Student B looks at picture B on page 78.

Now try to find the differences between the two pictures. Ask questions like: *Where's the Walkman?*

There are six differences between the pictures.

b Write down what the differences are.

Example:
In picture A the clothes are on the floor, but in picture B they are on the bed.

Asking for directions

Dominique *Excuse me. Where's the post office, please?*
English woman *It's opposite the ABC Cinema, between the Midland Bank and the chemist's.*
Dominique *Thanks very much.*
English woman *You're welcome.*

3 Where are they?

Look at the map at the top of page 15. Write complete sentences using the words and phrases below.

Example:
The post office is opposite the ABC Cinema.

1 ....
2 ....
3 ....
4 ....
5 ....
6 ....
7 ....
8 ....
9 ....
10 ....

```
opposite
between
next to
on the corner of
in . . .
on the right/left of . .
```

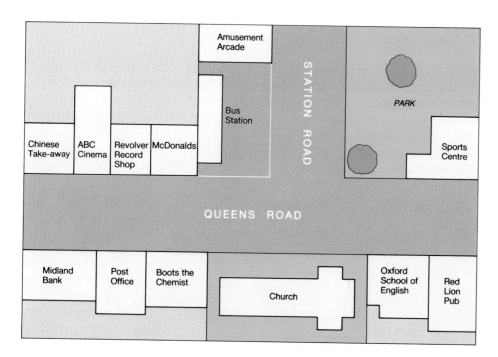

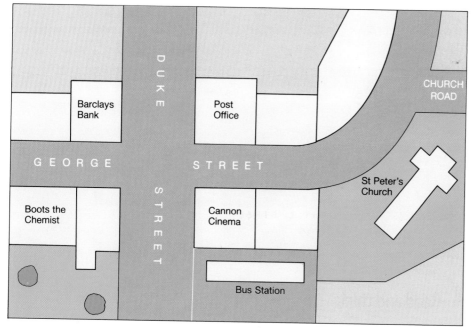

4 Ask and answer

a Work in pairs. Look at the map. Student A asks where a building or place is. Student B describes where it is. Then student B asks about another building or place, and student A answers.

Example:

A *Excuse me. Where's the bus station, please?*
B *It's on the corner of Queens Road and Station Road.*
A *Thanks very much.*
B *That's OK./You're welcome.*

b Ask and answer in the same way, using buildings and places in the town where you are.

5 Complete the maps

Work in pairs. Student A looks at the map opposite. Student B looks at the map on page 78.

Student A
You want to know where these places are:

1 the Queens Head pub
2 Ashton Park
3 the Pizza Hut
4 Shades disco
5 the Bombay Indian Take-away
6 C & A

Take it in turns to ask and answer. You start.

Summary of English in situations
• asking and describing where things are
• asking where places are
• thanking and responding to thanks

1 Sound right

a 🖭 Which word does not rhyme with the other two?

Example:

is (*trees*) *his*

The answer is 'trees' because it doesn't rhyme with 'is' and 'his'.

1 this   these   please
2 here   there   we're
3 where   near   pair
4 quite   right   quiet
5 or   four   hour
6 your   for   our
7 I'm   him   time
8 all   shall   call

b Now practise saying the sets of words above.

2 Work on words

What's the missing word? All the words are in units 1 and 2.

Example:
England/English   France/French

	England/English	France/French
1	a husband/Mr	a wife/...
2	I/my	we/...
3	he/his	she/...
4	this/here	that/...
5	14/fourteen	40/...
6	hello/hi	OK/...
7	right/left	above/...
8	Wednesday/a day	March/...
9	O/a circle	▢/...
10	—/a line	x/...
11	books/a bookcase	clothes/...
12	Steve/first name	Bond/...
13	all right/OK	cheerio/...
14	west/east	north/...
15	to drink/thirsty	to eat/...
16	Britain/a country	Hastings/...
17	Italy/Italian	Spain/...
18	Monday/today	Tuesday/...
19	1,000 m/1 km	100p/...
20	a car/cars	a bus/...

3 Listen to this

🖭 Listen to three short conversations. They all take place at the station. Follow the directions which you hear and draw lines on the map. Where does each person want to go to?

The first person wants to go to . . .
The second person wants to go to . . .
The third person wants to go to . . .

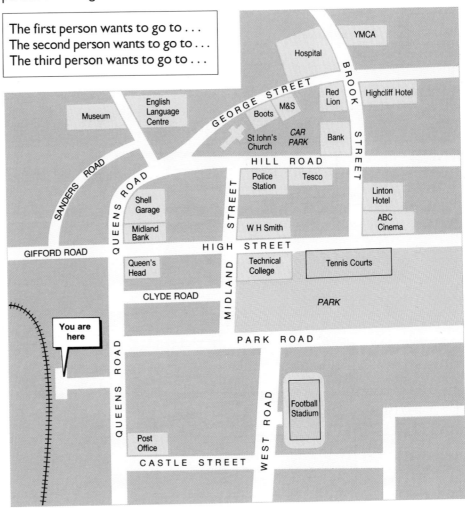

4 Read and think

There are eight people at a table. Read these clues and then write down who is who.

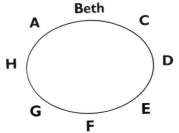

Tim is between Mark and Di.
Liz is opposite Di.
Nick is between Liz and Di.
Beth is between Kim and Liz.
Tim is opposite Beth.
Mark is on Tim's left.
Sue is on Kim's right.

A =   F =
C =   G =
D =   H =
E =

5 Play games in English

Make a word

Form teams of five students.
Each team writes five different letters
on five large pieces of paper.
Each student holds one letter.
The team stand in a line and make as
many words as they can in two
minutes.
A two-letter word gets 2 points, a
three-letter word 3 points, etc.
The team with the most points is the
winner.

6 Now you're here

British signs

What do these signs mean?
Where do you usually see them?
Ask a British person if necessary.

Things you buy

a Match the things on the left with
the shops on the right where you can
buy them.

aspirins
a newspaper
bananas   a chemist's
stamps
toothpaste
sweets   a newsagent's
a film
a magazine
suncream   a post office
apples
postcards
oranges   a greengrocer's
make-up

b Now think of other things you can
buy at a chemist's, a newsagent's and a
greengrocer's.

UNIT THREE

LESSON ONE

Rob meets Dominique

Hi Mum! Hi Dad! Where's the French girl?

Oh no!

We've got some bad news for you. Dominique's a boy.

This is Dominique.

Hello.

Hi. My name's Rob.

Half an hour later

Rob How old are you?

Dominique I'm sixteen. How about you?

Rob I'm fifteen.

Dominique Have you got any brothers or sisters?

Rob Yes, I've got a sister. She's at a friend's house at the moment.

Dominique What's she like?

Rob She's OK, but she's got a terrible temper!

Dominique You're lucky! You've got a computer.

Rob Yes, it's an Amstrad. But I've only got a few games.

Dominique Have you got a moped?

Rob A moped? No, I haven't. Have you?

Dominique Yes, I've got a 50 cc Honda.

Rob *You're* lucky! I've only got an old bike!

1 Questions and answers

a Match the questions on the left with the answers on the right.

Example: 1 – d

1 Have Mr and Mrs Bond got some bad news for Rob?
2 Has Rob got a bike?
3 Has Dominique got a computer?
4 Has Rob's sister got a terrible temper?
5 Have Mr and Mrs Bond got three children?
6 Has Rob's sister got two brothers?
7 Has Dominique's bedroom got a wardrobe?

a) Yes, he has.
b) No, they haven't.
c) Yes, it has.
d) Yes, they have.
e) No, he hasn't.
f) Yes, she has.
g) No, she hasn't.

b Work in pairs. Student A asks the same questions, Student B answers them without looking at the answers above. Change roles.

2 What have you got?

a Fill in the box with information about yourself.

		You	Your partner (B)
Have you got	a brother?		
	a sister?		
	a bike?		
	a moped?		
	a computer?		
	a radio?		
	an alarm clock?		

b Ask another student (B) about the things he/she's got and fill in the box.

Examples:
You *Have you got a brother?*
B *Yes, I have.*
You *Have you got a bike?*
B *No, I haven't.*

c Write five sentences about yourself and student B.

Examples:
I've got a bike but I haven't got a moped.
Pia's got a brother but she hasn't got a sister.

3 What are they?

a Work in pairs. Student A chooses a word from the list and asks, for example:
What's an Amstrad?
Student B answers with an adjective of nationality, like this:
It's a British computer.

Mercedes Benz	cricket	champagne
Rio de Janeiro	Hastings	SAAB
Oldsmobile	Bombay	koala bear
Coca Cola	vodka	Juventus
Alfa Romeo	Pentax	Toyota
Valencia	Lyon	Milan

b Write down some other things from different countries. Ask each other about them.

4 The things you've got

a Make a list of the things you've got in your pockets or bag.

Examples:
a comb, a pen, a passport, a wallet

b Talk to the student next to you. Find out what you've *both* got.

Example:
A *Have you got a comb in your bag?*
B *Yes, I have.*
A *I have, too.*

5 Quick questions

Go round the class asking questions. Find a student who:

	Name
hasn't got a brother has got a Walkman hasn't got a Japanese watch has got a tennis racket hasn't got a camera has got an umbrella	

Ask questions like this:
Have you got a brother?
The winner is the student who collects six names first.

6 Tell a lie

a Write four sentences about your brothers/sisters/the things you've got. Three sentences must be true, one must be a lie.

Example:
I've got one brother.
I haven't got a sister.
I've got a bike.
I haven't got a moped.

b Read your four sentences to the class. They must guess which one is a lie.

Grammar summary: page 82

19

1 The alphabet

Listen and repeat the letters of the alphabet.

2 What's the word?

Write down the letters you hear. What words do they make?

Example:
B-O-Y   Boy

1 ....
2 ....
3 ....
4 ....
5 ....
6 ....
7 ....
8 ....
9 ....
10 ....

3 Act it out

Practise the following dialogue in pairs, using your own address in Britain.
Say 'Sorry?' if you don't understand what your partner says. Change roles.

Spelling in English

Dominique *Mrs Bond, what's your full address?*
Mrs Bond *9, Cornwallis Gardens.*
Dominique *Sorry?*
Mrs Bond *9, Cornwallis Gardens.*
Dominique *How do you spell Cornwallis?*
Mrs Bond *C-O-R-N-W-A-L-L-I-S.*
Dominique *And what's your postcode?*
Mrs Bond *TN34 6JW.*

4 Spelling game

Form two teams. Ask each other how to spell English words.

5 How to use a payphone

Match the following instructions with the pictures, and fill in the blanks next to the pictures.

- Don't forget to take your unused coins back.
- Put in your money.
- Pick up the receiver and listen for the dialling tone.
- Dial the number you want.
- Speak when somebody answers.
- Have your money ready (10p, 50p, £1).

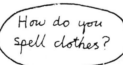

How do you spell clothes?

c - l - o . . .

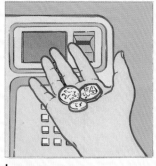

1 ....

2 ....

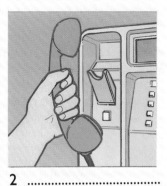

3 ....

4 ....

5 ....

6 ....

6 How to make an international phone call

1 Dial 010.
2 Then dial the code for your country.
Examples:
France 33, Italy 39, Japan 81, Brazil 55, West Germany 49

3 Now dial the code for the town or city you want *without* the first number.
Examples:
Stockholm 8, Madrid 1
4 Finally, dial the number of the person you want to speak to.

Now write down the full number of your family or a friend if you want to phone them from Britain.

010	34	1	4476807
International code	Country code (Spain)	City code (Madrid)	Number of family, friend, etc.

Summary of English in situations

- spelling
- asking someone to repeat something
- using a payphone and making an international phone call

21

1 Sound right

a 🔊 Listen to these pairs of words. What is the difference in pronunciation between the words on the left and the words on the right?

this	these
it	eat
hit	heat
sit	seat
fill	feel
live	leave
ship	sheep
will	wheel

b Now listen again and repeat the words.

c Choose six of the words above. Write them in boxes, like this:

sit	feel	ship
it	seat	live

d Listen to the teacher when he/she reads out words from the two lists above. Cross out your words when you hear them, like this:

~~sit~~	~~feel~~	~~ship~~
~~it~~	~~seat~~	~~live~~

e When all your words are crossed out, shout BINGO!

2 Work on words

Odd one out

Which of the four sums has a different answer?

3 Listen to this

🔊 Listen to the conversations. Which conversation goes with which picture?

a . . .

b . . .

c . . .

d . . .

e . . .

f . . .

A	1 eleven − three	B	1 seven + twelve	C	1 three × five	D	1 eighty-four ÷ three
	2 four × two		2 twenty-one − two		2 thirteen + two		2 forty − twelve
	3 sixty-four ÷ eight		3 three × six		3 sixty ÷ four		3 fourteen + fifteen
	4 six + three		4 fifty-seven ÷ three		4 twenty − six		4 seven × four

4 Read and think

Who's who?

a Read these descriptions of four men.

b Match the descriptions with the pictures below.

A's about thirty. He's quite tall and thin. He's got straight black hair. It's quite long. He's got a moustache.

B's about forty. He's not very tall, but he's quite heavy. He's got curly black hair, and a beard.

C's about thirty-five. He wears glasses. He's got brown hair but he hasn't got much of it left – he's almost bald.
He's of medium height and build.

D's about forty-five. He's got short grey hair and a grey moustache. He wears glasses. He's short and fat.

C Now write a similar description of a person you know.

5 Play games in English

Hangman

One student thinks of an English word. He/she writes a dash (−) on the board for each letter of the word.

Example:
COMPUTER = _ _ _ _ _ _ _ _

The other students then say one letter at a time. If the letter is in the word, the student at the board fills in the letter(s).

If the letter is not in the word, the student at the board draws one line of this picture:

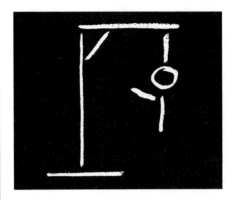

Students' right letters so far:
_ o _ _ u t _ _

Students' wrong letters so far:
s i a b n h w d

The students must try to guess the word before the man is 'hanged'.

6 Now you're here

a Ask a British person these questions and note down his/her answers.
You can practise the questions in class first.

- Have you got a passport? (How old is it?)
- Have you got a computer? (What kind is it?)
- Have you got any brothers or sisters? (What are their names?)
- Have you got a relative in a different country? (Which country is he/she in?)
- Have you got an old Beatles or Elvis Presley record? (Which one/s?)
- Have you got an English dictionary? (How big is it?)
- Have you got a typewriter? (What kind is it?)
- Have you got a boat? (Where is it?)
- Have you got a bicycle? (What make is it?)

b Compare the answers you get with other students' answers.

23

UNIT FOUR
LESSON ONE

💻 Do you like it?

Dominique What's this record?
Debbie It's Razzmataz.
Dominique What does that mean?
Debbie It doesn't mean anything. Do you like it?
Dominique It's all right.
Debbie What do you mean 'It's all right'? It's fantastic!!
Dominique Is it?
Debbie Yes, and Rob likes it too.
Dominique Does he?
Debbie Yes, he's got the record. What kind of music do you like, Dominique?
Dominique I like French music.
Debbie What do you mean, 'French music'?
Dominique Pop music with French singers and French words.
Debbie Do you have pop music in France?
Dominique Huh – of course we do. I've got a cassette in my room. Do you want to hear it?
Debbie Um . . . not now . . . um . . . I haven't got time.

I Questions and answers

a Complete the questions and answers with *do/does/don't* or *doesn't*.

Example:
Does Debbie like pop music? Yes, she does.

1 . . . Debbie like Razzmataz?
2 . . . Razzmataz mean 'fantastic'?
3 . . . Debbie and Rob like pop music?
4 . . . Dominique think Razzmataz is fantastic?
5 . . . Dominique like French music?
6 . . . Debbie and Rob know any French pop songs?
7 . . . Debbie want to listen to Dominique's cassette?

b Work in pairs. Student A asks the questions. Student B answers them without looking in the book.

2 Do you like . . . ?

a Fill in your answers to the questions in the table.

√ = Yes, I do.
x = No, I don't.
o = It's/They're OK.

b Work in pairs. Ask and answer questions like this:

You *Do you like pop music?*
A   *Yes, I do.*

c Write four sentences about yourself.

Examples:
I like hamburgers.
I don't like the winter.

d Write four sentences about Student A.

Examples:
He/She likes football.
He/She thinks this town is OK.

		You	A
Do you like	dancing?		
	football?		
	playing computer games?		
	hamburgers?		
	English coffee?		
	tea?		
	the winter?		
	this town?		
	learning English?		

3 A survey

a Write down the names of five pop groups/singers who all the class know.

b Form groups. Ask each other, 'Do you like . . .?'
Answer like this:

Yes, they're (he's/she's) fantastic.
(3 points)
Yes, they're (he's/she's) good.
(2 points)
They're (He's/She's) all right.
(I point)
No, they're (he's/she's) terrible.
(0 point)

One student in each group writes down the points and adds up the total.

c Work out which is the most popular group or the most popular singer.

4 Likes and dislikes

a Work in pairs. Student A looks at the information about Paul. Student B looks at the information about Carmen on page 78.

b Student A asks questions about the Spanish girl like this:

A *Does she like English pop music?*
B *Yes, she does.*

Student A fills in the missing information about her.

c Change roles. Student B asks questions about Paul.

Paul

English pop music: YES
English food: YES
Spanish food: NO
English weather: NO

Carmen

English pop music: . . .
English food: . . .
Spanish food: . . .
English weather: . . .

5 What does it mean?

a Form two teams. Team A asks team B questions like this about the words/phrases in the box. Choose only words or phrases you know:

A *What does 'auf wiedersehen' mean?*
B *It means 'goodbye' in German.*
(I point)

B *What does 'arrivederci' mean?*
A *It means 'come here' in Portuguese.*
(0 points)

buenos días   au revoir   si   ciao
bonjour   oui   mañana   nein
Autobahn   njet   uno, due, tre
ich liebe dich
siesta   je t'aime   bambino

b Think of other foreign words or phrases. Ask the other team what they mean, in the same way.

Grammar summary: page 83

25

📷 Telling the time

Debbie *What's the time?*
Dominique *Sorry?*
Debbie *What time is it?*
Dominique *It's five to five.*
Debbie *Oh no!*
Dominique *What's the matter?*
Debbie *Can you turn on the radio, please?*
Dominique *Why?*
Debbie *I want to listen to the new Top 40.*
Dominique *Pardon?*
Debbie *The Top 40—you know, this week's charts.*
Dominique *I'm sorry, I don't understand.*
Debbie *Oh, you're hopeless, Dominique! I haven't got time to explain. Just turn on the radio, quick!*

1 Times

📷 Listen to these times and write them down.

Example:
Twenty past five = 5.20

1 ....
2 ....
3 ....
4 ....
5 ....
6 ....
7 ....
8 ....
9 ....
10 ....

2 What's the time?

Work in pairs. Take turns to ask and say what time it is.

a

b

c

d

e

f

g

3 Dominique's timetable

9.00 – 10.00   'Grammar in action'
10.00 – 10.15   Break
10.15 – 11.15   'English in situations'
11.15 – 11.30   Break
11.30 – 12.30   'Fun with English'

Now ask each other when Dominique's lessons start and end.

Example:
A *What time does 'Grammar in action' start?*
B *It starts at nine (o'clock).*

4 What's missing?

Work in pairs. Student A looks at the list of programmes on Radio 1 on this page. Student B looks at the list of programmes on page 79. Ask each other questions, and fill in the missing information on your page.

Example:
What time does Adrian John's show start? What's on at 9.30?

TUESDAY

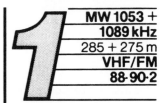

	MW 1053 +
	1089 kHz
	285 + 275 m
	VHF/FM
	88·90·2

VHF/FM Stereo between 10.0pm and 12 midnight
News on the half hour from 6.30am until 8.30pm, then 10.0 and 12 midnight

☐   **Adrian John**

7.0   Simon Mayo
with the **Breakfast Show**. Just before **8.0**, an exclusive preview of the new Top 40.

9.30 ☐

11.0   The Radio 1 Roadshow

with **Mike Read** at Portobello Beach, Edinburgh

☐   **Newsbeat**
with **Frank Partridge**

12.45   Gary Davies
with this week's Top 40

3.0 ☐

5.30   Newsbeat
with **Frank Partridge**

☐   **Peter Powell**
At **6.30** Peter reviews the new Top 40 singles.

7.30   Robbie Vincent
with special guests

10.0-12.0 ☐

5 Can you . . . please?

Work in pairs. Ask and answer like this:

1 pass

A *Can you pass the salt, please?*
B *Yes, all right. / OK.*

2 open

3 shut

4 turn on

What to say at mealtimes

Dominique *Can you pass the salt, please, Rob?*
Rob *Yes, here you are.*
Mrs Bond *Do you like it, Dominique?*
Dominique *Er . . . yes, it's very nice.*

(Five minutes later)

Mrs Bond *Would you like some more, Dominique?*
Dominique *No thanks, Mrs Bond, I'm full.*
Mrs Bond *Do you want some ice-cream?*
Dominique *Yes, please.*

5 answer

6 tidy

6 Would you like . . .?

a Work in pairs. Ask and answer questions like this:

Would you like some ice-cream?
Yes, please. / No, thank you.

meat	a pear
peas	an apple
gravy	sprouts

b Ask and answer questions in the same way. Use your own ideas.

Example:
Would you like some ketchup?

Summary of English in situations

- telling the time
- making requests
- making offers
- accepting and refusing food

27

1 Sound right

a 🎧 Listen to these pairs of words. What is the difference in pronunciation between the words on the left and the words on the right?

cat	cut
hat	hut
match	much
cap	cup
bat	but
ran	run
sang	sung

b Now listen again and repeat the words.

c Now tick (√) the words you hear.

1 but ☐   2 ran ☐
  bat ☐   run ☐

3 cat ☐   4 much ☐
  cut ☐   match ☐

5 cup ☐   6 sung ☐
  cap ☐   sang ☐

7 hat ☐
  hut ☐

d Work in pairs. Student A writes down seven of the words from the lists above. He/she then reads them out to student B.
Student B writes them down.
Student A and B compare their two lists. Change roles.

2 Listen to this

🎧 Listen to the three interviews.
Fill in the missing information in the table below with one of these symbols: √ o x

√ = he/she likes it
o = he/she thinks it's OK
x = he/she doesn't like it

		Pop music	Football	Modern fashion
	√	o	x	
Gary Carter				
Sandra Brent				
Charles Wentworth-Smythe				

3 Play games in English

Word tennis

Form two teams. The teacher chooses a category, for example:
food, transport, relatives, sport, weather.

Team A calls out one word in the category. Team B must say another word in the same category in only five seconds. The game goes on until one team can't think of another word in that category.

4 Work on words

a What is the odd word out in the following groups of words?

Example:

orange

banana

potato

apple

'Potato' is the odd word out because it is a vegetable. The other three are fruits.

1	French	7	tennis
	Spanish		squash
	Italy		football
	German		badminton
2	husband	8	park
	brother		pub
	sister		church
	father		bank
3	hi	9	record
	cheerio		computer
	goodbye		tape
	bye		cassette
4	ugly	10	chips
	beautiful		hamburger
	attractive		hot dog
	pretty		milk
5	bike	11	OK
	moped		terrible
	motorcycle		fine
	car		all right
6	doctor	12	salt
	dentist		pepper
	student		crisps
	teacher		ketchup

b Now explain why the odd word out is different from the other three.

5 Read and think

Read the story below. What do you think the man says in the last picture? Choose from a) b) c) or d).

A man goes into a restaurant. The waiter is surprised because the man has got boxing gloves on.

The man orders the most expensive things on the menu.

It's difficult for the man to eat and drink with his boxing gloves on.

The man eats an enormous meal, and then drinks a bottle of champagne.

The man finishes his meal, and asks for the bill.

Which is the best answer?

a) 'Because I'm a boxer.'
b) 'Because my hands are cold.'
c) 'Because I can't hold a knife and fork without them.'
d) 'Because I haven't got any money to pay the bill!'

6 Now you're here

a Ask a British person the following questions and note down his/her answers.
You can practise the questions in class first.

- Do you like fish and chips?
- Do you like champagne?
- Do you like cricket?
- Do you like boxing?
- Do you like jogging?
- Do you like pubs?
- Do you like dogs?
- Do you like pop music?
- Do you like classical music?

b Tell other students your most interesting answers.

UNIT FIVE

LESSON ONE

The problem with parents is . . .

Rob What's your mother like, Dominique?

Dominique She's OK, but she always asks my friends too many questions. She wants to know everything about them. 'Where do you live?' she asks. 'What does your father do?', 'Does your mother work?', and 'Where do you go for your holidays?', and so on and so on. It's so embarrassing!

Debbie What about your father?

Dominique He's all right, but he's got one really terrible habit.

Debbie What does he do?

Dominique He sings!

Debbie What's so terrible about that?

Dominique Well, he doesn't just sing in the bath. He sings when my friends are in the house, and his voice is so bad!

Rob Dad's got a really terrible habit too. He never remembers the names of my friends. But when they come to our house, he doesn't just say 'Hello'. He says 'Hello Peter' when really his name is Paul, or 'Hi Katherine' when her name's Karen.

Debbie Ummm, he sometimes embarrasses me too.

Dominique What does he do?

Debbie He wears jeans, tight jeans. He forgets he's nearly forty, not fourteen!

Rob Yes you're right. But what about Mum? Sometimes my friends come round and we talk about pop music. Then Mum comes in. She doesn't know anything about modern music, so she talks about the Beatles and the Rolling Stones instead!

Dominique But does she dance to the music too? My mother does, and that's *really* embarrassing!

I Make true sentences

Make true sentences from the table.

Example:
Debbie's mother likes the Rolling Stones.

Rob's father	(like)	her.
	(sing)	people's names.
Dominique's father	(wear)	a terrible voice.
	(have got)	tight jeans.
Debbie's mother	(dance)	in the bath.
	(forget)	too many questions.
Dominique's mother	(want)	to his records.
	(embarrass)	to know about his friends.
	(ask)	the Rolling Stones.

2 Ask and answer

a Work in pairs. Ask and answer questions.

Example:
mother / like pop music?
A *Does your mother like pop music?*
B *Yes, she does. (No, she doesn't.)*

1 father / sing in the bath?
2 father / wear tight jeans?
3 parents / like pop music?
4 mother / ask too many questions?
5 father / sing badly?
6 mother / dance well?
7 parents / embarrass you?
8 father / forget your friends' names?

b How do your parents embarrass you? Write three sentences about them.

c Compare your sentences in groups. Read out the most interesting examples to the rest of the class.

3 People's habits

a Work in pairs. Student A asks student B questions and fills in the table.

Example:
A *How often do you forget birthdays?*
B *I never forget birthdays.*

How often do you . . .?	always	often	sometimes	hardly ever	never
• forget birthdays?					✓
• sing in the bath?					
• dance?					
• go to church?					
• wear jeans?					
• listen to Beatles' records?					
• travel by train?					
• go to a disco?					

b Now write sentences like this about your partner:
' *He / She never forgets birthdays.*

c Tell the class about your partner.

Examples:
Claude never forgets birthdays.
He sometimes sings in the bath.

4 Girl meets boy

a Complete the girl's questions for the boy's answers.

Girl	Boy
• What . . .?	My name's Peter.
• Where . . .?	I live here in Hastings.
• How often . . .?	I come here every Saturday.
• What . . .?	I'm a student.
• Which . . .?	I go to East Hill School.
• What music . . .?	I like rock music.
• . . . dance?	Yes, OK.

b Practise the dialogue in pairs, but think of your own answers to the questions.

5 Tell a lie

a Write down four things about yourself. Three must be true and one must be a lie.

b Read out your sentences to the class. They must guess which one is the lie.

Examples:
I never wear jeans.
I like classical music.
My mother's 42.
I often forget birthdays.

Grammar summary: page 83

31

1 How much is this?

a Work in pairs. Point to the pictures and ask each other questions.

Example:
A *How much is this?*
B *It's 27p.*

1

2

3

4

5

b Now do the same with your own English money.

2 The money game

Look at these prices. What is the minimum number of coins you need to buy these things?

Example: 37p
4 coins – 20p 10p 5p 2p

1 16p   2 23p   3 20p

4 £3.95   5 £1.49   6 £1.89

3 How much is it?

Work in pairs. Student A chooses one of the things above and asks how much it is. Student B tells him/her.

Example:
A *How much is a can of Coke, please?*
B *37p.*

4 How much are they?

Work in pairs. Student A asks for two of the things above, student B says how much they cost.

Example:
A *Can I have a can of Coke and a packet of crisps, please?*
B *That's 57p, please.*

5 What's missing?

📺 Listen to this dialogue in a shop. Write down the prices of the things the girl buys, and then the total cost.

1 peanuts   . . . . .
2 bananas   . . . . .
3 milk chocolate . . . . .
4 lemonade   . . . . .

Total: . . . . .

6 What do you need?

Work in pairs. Student A is a customer and wants to buy four things for a picnic. Student B is a shopkeeper and tells student A what the things cost.

In a bank

Student Can I cash these traveller's cheques, please?

Bank clerk Yes. Have you got your passport, please?

Student Yes, here you are.

Bank clerk Can you sign the cheques, please?

Student Yes.

Bank clerk And can you fill in the date, please?

Student What is the date today?

Bank clerk It's the 10th. . . . How do you want the money?

Student Sorry?

Bank clerk Do you want it in fives or tens?

Student Fives, please.

7 Act it out

Practise the dialogue above in pairs. One of you is the student, the other is the bank clerk. You can also use your own ideas.

Summary of English in situations

- asking for things
- asking and talking about the cost of things

8 What's missing?

Work in pairs. Student A looks at the pictures and prices on this page. Student B looks at the pictures and prices on page 79. Ask and answer questions to find out the missing prices.

Examples:

B *How much do the shoes cost?*

A *They cost £35.99.*
   How much does the jacket cost?

B *It costs £49.50.*

1 Sound right

a 🎧 Listen to these words from the dialogue on page 30.

problem	habit
question	remember
everything	forget
holiday	fourteen
embarrassing	forty
terrible	music

b Now listen again. Which syllable (part of the word) do you say most strongly or heavily? Underline that syllable, like this:

<u>pro</u>blem

c Now read the words. Say the syllables you underlined as strongly or heavily as possible.

2 Play games in English

Word chain

Form two teams.
The teacher writes a word in the top left-hand corner of the board (for example: HABIT).
One member of team A adds another word beginning with the last letter of the first word (for example: TERRIBLE). Time limit: 30 seconds.
Then one member of team B adds another word beginning with E, and so on.
You get 3 points for a 3-letter word, 4 points for a 4-letter word, etc.

3 Listen to this

a 🎧 Nicola Adams is a friend of Rob's. Listen to what she does every morning. Look at the pictures and fill in the times when she does different things.

1 ....

2 ....

3 ....

4 ....

5 ....

6 ....

b Now write down what Nicola does in each picture.
Use the words in the box.

have breakfast	leave home
catch a bus	get up
have a shower	get dressed

Example:
She gets up at half past seven.

1	4 ....
2	5 ....
3	6 ....

4 Read and think

a Read about which foods these four people like and don't like.

Adam   Beth   Clare   Linda

- Adam likes fish but he doesn't like chips.
- Beth doesn't like fish or hot dogs.
- Clare only likes the same things as Adam.
- Linda likes three things.
- Beth only likes one thing—the thing which Linda doesn't like.
- Clare likes hot dogs.
- Chips aren't the only thing which Adam doesn't like.
- Linda doesn't like hamburgers.

Now answer these questions:

1 Does Adam like hot dogs?
2 Does Clare like chips?
3 Does Linda like fish?
4 Does Beth like hamburgers?
5 Does Clare like fish?
6 Does Linda like hot dogs?
7 Does Adam like hamburgers?
8 Does Beth like chips?

b Look at the picture again and 'give' each person something that he/she likes.

5 Work on words

a Match the verbs on the left with the words on the right.

Example:
You speak English.

You		
	1 ask	a) a bus
	2 eat	b) jeans
	3 speak	c) a question
	4 wear	d) a hamburger
	5 catch	e) the radio
	6 listen to	f) games
	7 play	g) English
	8 ride	h) a door
	9 read	i) a bike
	10 drink	j) a magazine
	11 open	k) a cheque
	12 cash	l) coffee

b Now think of other words to go with the verbs on the left.

Example:
You listen to a record.

6 Now you're here

a Ask a British person these questions.

- What time do you get up?
- What do you have for breakfast?
- What time do you usually have lunch?
- Where do you have lunch?
- How many cups of tea do you usually drink a day?
- What time do you usually go to bed?
- Which newspaper do you read?
- Which television channel do you watch most?
- Which radio station do you listen to most?
- Where do you usually go on holiday?
- How often do you . . .
    go to the cinema?
    eat in a restaurant?
    go to a pub?
    go to the hairdresser's?
    go abroad?
    go to the dentist's?

b Tell the rest of the class about the most interesting answers.

UNIT SIX · LESSON ONE

GRAMMAR IN ACTION

On the beach

Sammy Hey, have you got the time?
Dominique No, I'm sorry, I haven't.
Sammy You're not English, are you?
Dominique Can you hear my accent?
Sammy Yes, of course I can.
Dominique Where am I from? Can you guess?
Sammy Spain?
Dominique No.
Sammy Italy?
Dominique No. Wrong again.
Sammy Are you French?
Dominique Yes, of course I am.
Sammy What a pity.
Dominique Why? What's the problem?
Sammy I can't speak French.
Dominique No problem. I can speak a bit of English.
Sammy But I can't understand your English.
Dominique Can't you?

Sammy Don't worry. I can really. Come on! Let's have a swim.
Dominique No, thanks.
Sammy Why not?
Dominique I can't swim!

1 Questions and answers

a Match the questions on the left with the answers on the right.

Example: 1 – h

1 Is Dominique French?	a) Yes, she is.
2 Can he speak English?	b) Yes, she does.
3 Can Sammy understand Dominique's English?	c) Yes, he has.
4 Is Sammy English?	d) Yes, a bit.
5 Can Dominique swim?	e) No, she hasn't.
6 Has Sammy got a watch?	f) No, he can't.
7 Does Sammy speak to Dominique first?	g) Yes, she can.
8 Has Dominique got a French accent?	h) Yes, he is.

b Work in pairs. Student A asks the same questions. Student B answers them without looking in the book. Change roles.

2 Write it again

a Work in pairs. Re-write the dialogue between Dominique and Sammy. This time Dominique speaks to Sammy first.
Student A writes what Dominique says first, and then passes it to student B. Student B writes what Sammy says in reply.
Write four or five lines each. The dialogue you write can be completely different from the one in the book.

b Practise your dialogue together.

c Act it out in class.

3 Ask a friend

a Work in pairs. Look at the pictures and ask and answer questions about them like this:
A *Can you swim?*
B *Yes, I can. / No, I can't. / Yes, I can a bit.*

Choose from the verbs in the box.

swim	type	ski
skateboard	windsurf	drive

b Write sentences about your partner.

Examples:
He / She can play tennis.
He / She can't windsurf.
He / She can skateboard a bit.

c Tell the rest of the class about your partner.

4 Can they or can't they?

a Ask other students in the class the same questions as in exercise 3. Ask each student only *one* question.

b Write down the names of the students you speak to and their answers, like this.

Examples:
Juan – swim	Yes
Pia – ski	No
Marco – windsurf	No

Continue until you have got three 'Yes' answers and three 'No' answers.

c The teacher names a student in the class. The rest of the class tell the teacher about the student, like this:

Teacher	*Juan.*
Student 1	*He can swim.*
Student 2	*He can't windsurf.*
Student 3	*He can ski.*

d Write down three other things you can do. Then tell the class about them.

5 Speak to Sammy

Complete this dialogue between Sammy and yourself.

Sammy *Have you got the time?*
You ....
Sammy *You're not English, are you?*
You ....
Sammy *Where are you from?*
You ....
Sammy *How much English can you understand?*
You ....
Sammy *How much English can you speak?*
You ....
Sammy *Why are you here in England?*
You ....
Sammy *How long are you here for?*
You ....

Grammar summary: page 83

Rules of the house

① You must be on time for meals

② You must come home before 11 o'clock

③ You mustn't smoke in your room .....

④ You mustn't use the telephone without permission

⑤ You must ask permission before you have a bath

⑥ You mustn't play music too loudly

⑦ You mustn't have friends in your room

1 The rules of your house

Tick (√) those rules above which are true in your family in Britain or in your family at home. Compare your answers.

2 Can they or can't they?

Listen to these foreign students talking about their English families. Mark the things they can do with a tick (√), and the things they mustn't/can't do with a cross (×).

	come home late?	smoke in his/her room?	have a bath every day?	have friends in his/her room?
Marco				
Pia				
Martine				
Takao				

3 Can you or can't you?

Ask other students questions about the rules in their houses.

Ask and answer questions like this:
A *Can you come home after 11 o'clock?*
B *No, I can't.*

Mark the answers with a tick (√) for yes or a cross (×) for no.

Can you . . .

be late for meals? ☐
come home after 11 o'clock? ☐
smoke in your room? ☐
use the telephone without permission? ☐
have a bath without permission? ☐
play loud music in your room? ☐
have friends in your room? ☐

4 Mini dialogue

Practise this dialogue in pairs.

A *Can I use the telephone, please?*
B *Yes, of course./No, I'm afraid you can't.*

Now student A should use the words below instead of the underlined words:

have a bath
come home after eleven
smoke in my room
be late for dinner.

Change roles. Practise more dialogues using your own ideas.

5 Role play

Work in pairs. Act out the dialogues in these situations.

6 What do they mean?

Work in pairs. Student A points at a sign or notice and asks, 'What does this mean?' Student B answers.

Example:
A *What does this sign mean?*
B *It means you must queue on this side of the sign.*
    or
You mustn't queue on the other side of the sign.

7 Find your own

Write down more examples of notices or signs you have seen. Ask your teacher or other students in the class, 'What does this mean?'

Summary of English in situations

● talking about rules and obligations

1 Sound right

a How do you pronounce the names of these companies and products in your language?

Coca-Cola
Kodak
Honda
McDonalds
Renault
Philips
Esso
Marlboro
Avis

Pan Am
Hilton Hotel
Mercedes Benz
Texaco
Rolls Royce
Sanyo
Pepsi-Cola
Citroën
Xerox

b ▣ Now listen to how they sound in English.

c Listen again and repeat. In what ways is the English pronunciation different from yours?

d Work in groups. Think of other international companies / products. Try to pronounce them in an English way. Check your pronunciation with your teacher.

2 Listen to this

a ▣ Listen to the instructions on the cassette and do exactly what the voice tells you to do.

b Work in pairs. Give each other instructions. Use the following verbs and the parts of the body in exercise 3.

open	close	touch
turn	put	pull
shake	stand	fold

3 Work on words

a Choose the right words from the box to label the parts of the body.

| arm | head | eye | mouth | foot | stomach | hand |
| ear | leg | finger | nose | hair | toe | |

b Now work in pairs. Student A points to a part of his/her body, and student B says what it is in English.

4 Read and think

a Look at this cartoon story.

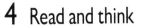

b Now read what the men say. The sentences are not in the right order.

a) 'HELP!! WATER . . . WATER!!'
b) 'I've got blue ties, red ties, green ties. . . . Which one do you want?'
c) 'I don't believe it! A restaurant – in the middle of the desert!'
d) 'It's so hot. I must find some water.'
e) 'No, I'm sorry. I haven't got any water. But I've got some ties.'
f) 'Have you got any water? I'm very thirsty.'
g) 'Ties? I don't want a tie. I want water!'
h) 'I'm sorry sir. You can't come into this restaurant without a tie!'

c Now decide where each of the sentences goes in the cartoon story. Put the right letter into the speech bubbles.

d Now re-tell the story. Use the verbs in the box if you want to.

crash	survive	look for
meet	ask	say
try	sell	go on
see	speak	tell

5 Play games in English

Help 'the blind'

One student goes out of the room. The other students change the position of the table and chairs in the room. The teacher blindfolds the student outside the room. He/she comes back into the room. The other students give him/her instructions like these:

Go straight on. Stop!

Take one step to the left.

Turn right.

Go forwards (backwards) one step.

The idea is to guide the 'blind' student from one side of the room to the other without touching anything.

6 Now you're here

a Ask a British person these questions and note down his/her answers.

- Can you speak French/German/Spanish? (How well can you speak it/them?)
- Can you swim? (Can you swim butterfly?)
- Can you type? (How many fingers do you use?)
- Can you ride a motorbike?
- Can you play chess? (How well can you play?)
- Can you play the piano? (How well can you play it?)
- Can you ski?
- Can you skate?
- Can you windsurf?
- Can you dance the waltz?
- Can you knit?
- Can you make a cake?

b Tell other students your most interesting answers.

41

GRAMMAR IN ACTION

I'm busy

No, I'm sorry, I can't. I'm peeling the potatoes.

Where's Rob?

He's upstairs, in his room.

Steve, what are you doing? Can you lay the table, please?

What's he doing?

He's probably listening to music, as usual.

Well, what about Debbie?

I don't know. Why don't you ask her?

Debbie! What are you doing? Debbie . . . where are you?

I'm in the bathroom. I'm having a shower.

Oh no!

Can I help you?

No, you're busy—you're writing a letter.

No, it's all right.

Oh, thank you, Dominique. You *are* kind.

No, I'm not— I'm starving!

1 Questions and answers

a Write six questions and answers from the table.

Example:
Is Mr Bond peeling the potatoes? Yes, he is.

Is	Mr Bond Mrs Bond Mr and Mrs Bond	peeling the potatoes? laying the table? writing a letter?	Yes,	he	is (n't).
Are	Debbie Dominique Rob Debbie and Rob	having a shower? listening to music? working?	No,	she they	are (n't).

b Work in pairs. Student A asks his/her questions. Student B answers them.

c Student B asks the questions, Student A answers them.

d Think of more questions about what is happening in the pictures. Ask and answer your questions in pairs.

2 Dominique's postcard

Dominique's got an American pen-friend. He's writing a postcard to her. He's describing what's happening around him, what he's doing, etc. Write the postcard, using the information in the picture.

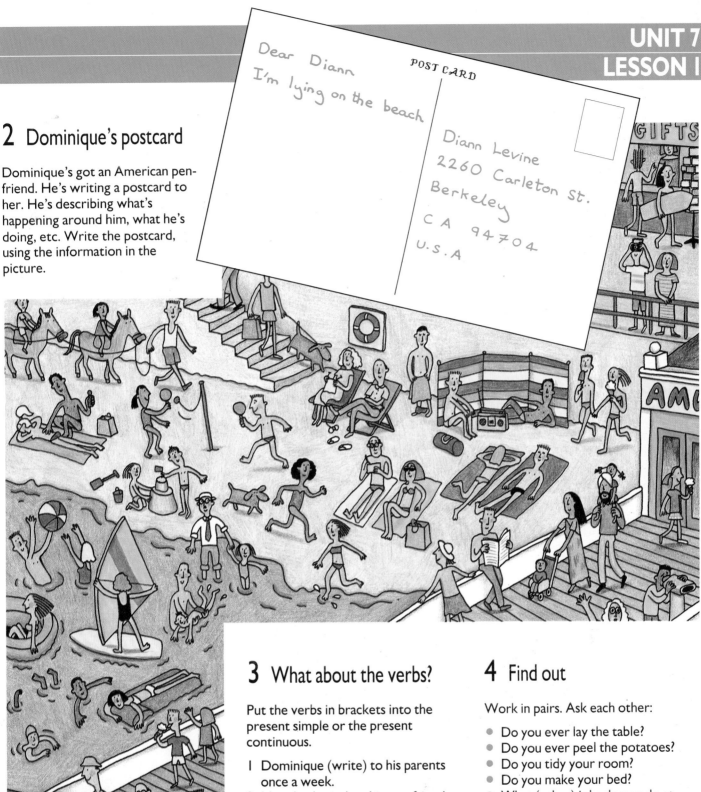

Dear Diann
I'm lying on the beach

POST CARD

Diann Levine
2260 Carleton St.
Berkeley
CA 94704
U.S.A

3 What about the verbs?

Put the verbs in brackets into the present simple or the present continuous.

1 Dominique (write) to his parents once a week.
2 Now he (write) to his pen-friend.
3 Debbie (wash) her hair three times a week.
4 It (rain). It often (rain) in England.
5 I can't answer the phone. I (have) a shower.
6 Dominique (speak) quite good English, but Rob (not speak) French.
7 What programme you (watch)? A Clint Eastwood film.
8 What you (cook)? I (starve)!

4 Find out

Work in pairs. Ask each other:

- Do you ever lay the table?
- Do you ever peel the potatoes?
- Do you tidy your room?
- Do you make your bed?
- What (other) jobs do you do at home?
- How often do you write letters / postcards?
- How often do you have a shower / bath?
- What do you think your mother / father / sister / brother is doing now?
- Is it raining?

Grammar summary: page 84

What's your telephone number?

Dominique *What's your telephone number, Mrs Bond?*
Mrs Bond *712660.*
Dominique *Sorry, what do you mean – double six?*
Mrs Bond *Six six.*
Dominique *And what does 'oh' mean?*
Mrs Bond *It means zero.*

1 Telephone numbers

Write down the telephone numbers you hear.

1 ....
2 ....
3 ....
4 ....
5 ....
6 ....

2 Quick questions

Go round the class and ask each other, 'What's your telephone number?' Write down the student's name and the number. The winner is the student with the most correct telephone numbers after three minutes.

3 What's missing?

Work in pairs. Student A looks at the page from the Hastings telephone directory on this page. He/She then asks Student B for the missing information.

Example:
A *What's R.M. Bond's telephone number?*
B *Hastings 422952.*

Student B looks at the page from the Hastings telephone directory on page 80 and asks student A for the missing information.

881008	Bond J.R, 1 Surrender...	Tonbridge 36743 Bone
210633	Bond Kay, 18 Robertson Ho,Hastings Rd......	Tun Wells 36743 Bone
362786	Bond K, 42 Priory Rd	Tun Wells 22485 Bone
712718	Bond K.L, 19 Cavendish Dv	Tun Wells 28750 Bone
354564	Bond L.A, South Riding,Upper Cumberland Wlk	Bone
dge 673	Bond L.R, Leighton,Dower Ho Cres,Southborough	Bone
s 217591	Bond L.T,	Brede 882703 Bone
lls 42819	20 Gresham Wy,Filsham Pk,St. Leonards-o-s .	Hastings 437315 Bone
field 3626	Bond M, Sunnyside,Cackle St	Heathfield 2679 Bone
s 212151	Bond M, 2 Quarry Cres	Tun Wells 33214 Bone
tford 2789	Bond M.A, 7 Holly Clo,Hailsham Rd......	Burwash 883236 Bone
rden 2592	Bond N.C, 4 Earls Rd	Tun Wells 43297 Bon
nbury 2260	Bond Norman F.G, Linden,Swiffe La,Broad Oak	Forest Rw 3308 Bon
	Bond N.H, 13 Kendal Pk	Bon
	Bond N.J, Belnor,Chapel La......	Smallfield 2443 Bor
ings 422744	Bond P.D, 2 The Grange	Otford 4616 Bo
ings 754384	Bond P.E.T, 8 Grange Wy	Heathfield 2576 Bo
e Gn 830338	Bond P.F, 21a East Hill Fm,Kemsing	Burwash 882294 Bo
tings 441497	Bond R.A, Unit 14 Waldron Ct Mutton Hall Hill	Hastings 429077 Bo
stings 429843	Bond R.A, Roseneath,Shrub Rd	Copthorne 714586 B
tersham 380	Bond R.C, 166 Sedlescombe Rd Nth,St. Leonards-o-S ...	Fairseat 822889 B
gh Gn 884491	Bond R.G, 8 Woodland Clo,Crawley Dwn	
mans Pk 403	Bond R.H.C, Five Acres,Oakfarm La	Sevenoaks 452818
n Wells 34592	Bond R.M, 73 Edmund Rd	Tonbridge 361242
astings 712533	Bond Robert W, Ashgrove Cott,Gracious La	Westerham 62567
Hastings 52668	Bond S, 20 Rodney Av	Edenbridge 862780
Oxted 716714	Bond S.A, 57 Quebec Av	Hastings 712660
n Wells 510196	Bond S.E, 16 Sunnyside	Fairseat 823642
Hastings 753684	Bond S.G, 7/39 Cornwallis Gdns	W Malling 848105
tchingham 451	Bond S.W, 45 Timberbank,Meopham,Gravesend	
Crowboro 4996	Bond T, 11 Auden Rd,Larkfield	Tun Wells 41129
Etchingham 430	Bond T, 15 The Dene	Sharpthorne 810721
Oxted 712201	Bond T, 6 Vale Rd,Southborough......	
Hastings 813587	Bond T.C, 2 Warren Cotts,Stonelands,W Hoathly	E Grinstead 28632
Oxted 717562	Bond T.J, 8 Geary Pl,Westfield	Hastings 712242
Hawkhurst 2564	Bond T.P, 51 Forest View Rd	Bexhill-o-s 224220
taplehurst 892438	Bond V.C, 7 Reedswood Rd,St.Leonards-o-s......	Tenterden 2658
Sevenoaks 458060	Bond V.F, 1 New Brassey Ct,6,Brassey Rd	
Uckfield 2569	Bond W, 17 Heather Dv,St. Michaels	Cranbrook 712311
Buxted 3492	Bond W.F, 16 Keld Dv	Bexhill-o-s 218416
Crowboro 64110	Bond W.G, Pound Ho,Willsley Pound......	Rotherfield 2444
E Grinstead 28890	Bond William.J, 180 Ninfield Rd	
E Grinstead 314599	Bond W.W, Loft Cott 4 New Rd	Paddock Wd 346
Tonbridge 356862	Bondelivery Service Ltd –	
Rye 225222	29 Eldon Wy	Horam Rd 222
Crowboro 2815	Bonding Systems Ltd,Adhesives Mfrs,	Paddock Wd 346
Sandhurst 518	Vines Cross Rd,Horam ..	Tonbridge 3567
Cooden 4453		Tonbridge 3627
Biddenden 291813	Bond's Delivery Service, 29 Eldon Wy	Tonbridge 3513
Hastings 751739	Bonds E, 14 Lodge Rd	Oxted 7176
	Bonds G, 29 College Av	Sevenoaks 463
Borough Gn 882470	Bonds R.J, 81 Higham La......	Groombdge
Smallfield 2907	Bone A.N.G, 103 Home Pk,Hurst Gn	Newick 2
	Bone B.J, 14 Hurst Fm Road,Weald	Frittenden
Grinstead 25091	Bone C.A, Hamsell Manor Barn,Eridge	Hadlow 856
	Bone C.A, Fir Tree Cott,Station Rd	bridge 35
	Bone C.A, Parsonage Fm	

Speaking on the phone

Pam *Hello! 302 6517.*
Randy *Hello, can I speak to Sylvie, please?*
Pam *Yes, just a minute . . . Sylvie!*
Sylvie *Hello!*
Randy *Hi, Sylvie. It's Randy.*
Sylvie *Oh, hi Randy . . .*

4 Talking on the phone

In groups of three, practise the dialogue above. Use your own names and telephone numbers.

Taking a message

Phil *857 0099.*
Laura *Hello, can I speak to Mario please?*
Phil *No, I'm sorry, he's not in. Can I take a message?*
Laura *Yes, can you ask him to ring me tonight?*
Phil *OK, who's speaking?*
Laura *This is Laura.*
Phil *All right, Laura, I'll tell him.*
Laura *Thank you. Bye!*
Phil *Goodbye.*

5 Can I take a message?

Practise the dialogue in pairs. Use your own names and telephone numbers.

6 Telephone messages

Listen to these telephone conversations. Fill in the gaps in the messages.

MANOLO
RING - - - -
- - - - 8
HER NUMBER: - - -
- - - -

Mitsuko
Rang.
She has 2 tickets
for - - - - - tonight-
Starts - - - . Meet
her - - - - -
bus station
- - -

7 Act it out

In pairs, act out the two telephone conversations you heard in exercise 6. Use the messages you wrote to help you. You can also use your own ideas.

8 What's missing?

Work in pairs. Student A looks at the information below. Student B looks at the information on page 80.

Student A

You want to know:

where the concert is	. . . . .
what time it starts	. . . . .
what number bus to take	. . . . .
where to get off the bus	. . . . .
where Tiffany's is.	. . . . .

Student B knows the answers. Ask him/her your questions. Write down the information Student B gives you.

1 Sound right

a 🔊 Listen to these pairs of words.

1 ☐ sin   4 ☐ sank
   ☐ thin   ☐ thank
2 ☐ sink   5 ☐ sort
   ☐ think   ☐ thought
3 ☐ sick   6 ☐ some
   ☐ thick   ☐ thumb

b Listen again and repeat the words.

c Now listen and tick which word you hear.

d Listen to these pairs of words.

thin   tin
three   tree
thank   tank
thick   tick

e Listen and repeat the words.

f Draw six squares and write six of the words from the lists above in them.

Example:

sort	thin	some
tree	tick	thumb

g Listen to your teacher when he/she reads out words from the lists above. Cross out your words when you hear them.
When all your words are crossed out, shout BINGO!

2 Listen to this

🔊 Look at the picture below.

Now listen to a description of what is happening in the park.
Some of the things you hear are true, some are not true.
Write a tick (√) if the sentence is true, and a cross (×) if it is not true.

1 ....   6 ....
2 ....   7 ....
3 ....   8 ....
4 ....   9 ....
5 ....   10 ....

3 Read and think

a Follow the instructions below.

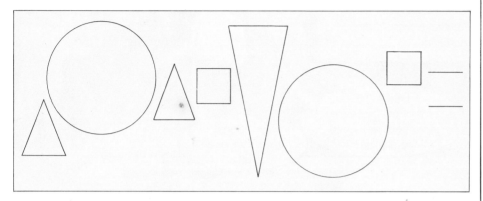

- First, write the number thirteen in the square between two triangles.
- Now draw a straight line under the triangle on the left.
- Then put a cross in the triangle which is on the left of the square with the number thirteen in it.
- Now write your first name in the circle between a triangle and a square.
- After that, join the two parallel lines to make a square.
- Now write today's date in that square.
- Then write your surname in the circle on the left.
- Now draw a small circle in the triangle to the left of the circle with your first name in it.
- Next, draw a line from the top of the triangle on the left to the middle of the line below it.
- Finally, write the answer to this sum in the empty square:
  thirteen − three + eighteen ÷ seven × twelve − six

b Work in pairs. Compare your answers.

c Now write your own instructions, like those above. Show them to your partner. He/She follows the instructions.

4 Work on words

Find words in the box on the right which mean the same or almost the same as the words in the box on the left.

Example:
hi   hello

to ring	to talk
all right	to get to
starving	bicycle
right	fantastic
hi	hello
to speak	hungry
to start	OK
to shut	to phone
quick	to close
pardon?	horrible
to arrive	nearly
toilet	large
terrible	until
dad	now
bike	a little
at the moment	fast
too	correct
almost	to begin
you're welcome	sorry?
a bit	not at all
great	father
famous	loo
big	also
to finish	well-known
till	to end

5 Play games in English

What am I doing?

a Form two teams. Think of actions which you can mime.

Examples:
eat spaghetti, watch tennis

b Team A write an instruction like the examples above, on a piece of paper.
One member of team B reads the instruction, goes to the front of the class and mimes it. His/her team try to guess what he/she is doing. They are only allowed three guesses.

Example:
'What am I doing?'
'You're eating spaghetti.'

c Team B writes an instruction on a piece of paper, and a member of team A mimes it to his/her team, etc.

6 Now you're here

a Find out the answers to these questions.

1 What time do banks open in the morning?
2 What time do pubs close at lunch-time?
3 Which day of the week do the shops in this town close early?
4 What number do you dial if you want to speak to the operator?
5 How much does it cost to send a first class letter in this country?
6 What's the price of a cinema ticket in this town?
7 What's the name of the local evening newspaper?
8 What programme's on BBC1 at nine o'clock tonight?
9 What's the dialling code for Manchester?
10 What's number one in the Top Forty at the moment?

b Compare your answers in class.

UNIT EIGHT · LESSON ONE

GRAMMAR IN ACTION

48

1 Make true sentences

Look at the pictures on page 48. Describe what is in them with the help of the table below.

At the barbecue there	's isn't are aren't	some any	English people. Coca-Cola. sausages. adults. ketchup. music. hamburgers. mustard. French students.

2 What's in the picture?

Look at picture A. Ask and answer questions in pairs using the words in the box below.

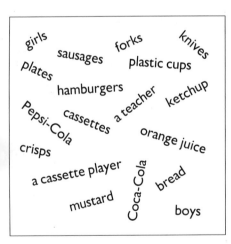

girls forks knives
sausages plastic cups
plates
hamburgers ketchup
cassettes a teacher
Pepsi-Cola orange juice
crisps
a cassette player bread
mustard Coca-Cola boys

Examples:
A *Are there any girls in the picture?*
B *Yes, there are.*
A *Is there any Pepsi-Cola?*
B *No, there isn't.*

3 Spot the differences

Look at picture B, and then at picture A in exercise 2. What differences can you see between them?
Describe the differences like this:
In picture A there's some orange juice. In picture B there isn't any.

A

B

4 How good is your memory?

a Form two teams.

b All the students in the class look around the classroom for one minute and try to remember everything in it.

c One member of each team goes out of the room.

d The two teams prepare questions like these:

How many girls are there in the room?
Is there a clock?
Are there any pictures on the walls?

e The two students come back into the room. They stand at the front with their backs to the class. The two teams ask each of them the same questions. Each correct answer gets one point for that student's team.

5 What happens next?

a Read the dialogue on page 36 again. Write the next six lines of the conversation between Sammy and Dominique.
Work in pairs. Student A writes what Dominique says. Student B writes what Sammy says. Write one line at a time.

b Practise reading your conversation in pairs.

c Act out your conversation in front of the class.

Grammar summary: page 84

49

I Invitations / offers

Work in pairs. Student A invites
student B to do the things in the
pictures.
Use the words under the pictures.

Start your sentences:
Would you like to . . . ?
Do you want to . . . ?

B answers:
Yes, please. / Yes, all right. / Yes, OK.

Change roles.

dance

sit down

play

get on

borrow

listen

swim

look at

2 Making excuses

Work in pairs. Student A invites student B to do the things in the pictures. Student B makes excuses.

Example:
A *Would you like to go to a concert?*
B *No thanks,* | *I've got a headache.*
I'm busy / tired.
I'm not feeling well.
I must do my homework.
I must write a letter.
I must wash my hair.

3 More excuses

Now practise inviting and making excuses in pairs, using your own ideas.

4 Sorry, I can't

🖼 Listen to the telephone conversation. Write T (true) or F (false) next to these sentences:

1 Sharon phones David.   . . . . .
2 Sharon remembers David.   . . . . .
3 There's a party at Sharon's.   . . . . .
4 Sharon can go to the party.   . . . . .
5 Sharon must wash her hair
   before she goes to the club.   . . . . .
6 David wants to see a film
   called *Yours For Ever*.   . . . . .
7 David wants to take Sharon
   to the cinema on Friday.   . . . . .

5 Role play

Work in pairs. Student A reads the information below. Student B looks at the information on page 80.

Situation 1
You want to go to the cinema with Student B. It's a horror film.
It starts at 8 o'clock. Phone student B and invite him / her. Try to persuade him / her to come!

Situation 2
Student B phones you and invites you to play tennis. You want to play but you're not free until 6 o'clock. Another problem is that you haven't got a tennis racket.

Summary of English in situations

- inviting and making offers
- accepting / refusing invitations and offers
- apologizing and making excuses

1 Sound right

a 🖭 Listen to these words.
Underline the syllables which you say
most strongly or heavily.

student	problem
later	another
over	cinema
horror	persuade
tired	different
mustard	tomorrow
letter	badminton
afraid	hamburger

b Now listen again and circle the
syllables which you say very quickly or
lightly.

Example:

student⟨⟩

What sound is in all of these syllables?

c Now listen and repeat the words.
Say the 'heavy' syllables as heavily as
possible, and the 'light' syllables as
lightly as possible.

2 Work on words

Write words which are opposites of
those on the left. Put one letter in
each box.

Example:

big   [s] [m] [a] [l] [l]

1 easy
2 same
3 above
4 cheap
5 late
6 full
7 dirty
8 noisy
9 never
10 thin
11 stupid
12 fast
13 last
14 tall
15 dry

3 Play games in English

The crossword game

a Form two teams. The teacher
draws two empty crosswords on the
board, like this:

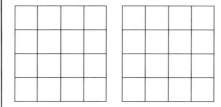

b One student from each of the
teams writes a word in his/her team's
crossword, across or down. You get 4
points for a 4-letter word, 3 points for
a 3-letter word, etc.

c The first two students give the pen
or chalk to two other students in their
teams who then write another word
in their crosswords.

d The game is over when all the
squares in the crosswords have been
filled, or when the teams can't think of
more words to write.
The teacher then adds up the total
points. The board can look like this:

H	A	N	D
A	N	D	O
R	O	A	O
D	R	Y	R

hand =	4	points
and =	3	points
dry =	3	points
hard =	4	points
an =	2	points
nor =	3	points
or =	2	points
day =	3	points
do =	2	points
door =	4	points

TOTAL: 30 points

4 Listen to this

a 🖭 Listen to a girl speaking on the
telephone to a boy.

b Now read these questions.

		Yes	No
1	Does Peter answer the phone?	☐	☐
2	Is Peter listening to the radio?	☐	☐
3	Is Peter watching *Eastenders*?	☐	☐
4	Does *Eastenders* finish at seven o'clock?	☐	☐
5	Does Peter want to go out with Becky?	☐	☐
6	Is Peter ready to go out?	☐	☐
7	Does Peter want Becky to come to his house?	☐	☐
8	Does Peter want to bring a friend with him?	☐	☐
9	Does Becky like Nick?	☐	☐

c Listen to the conversation on the
phone again and answer the questions.
Tick (√) the right answer.

d Now listen to the conversation
again. This time you can hear what
Peter says. Check your answers.

5 Read and think

This is a story in ten parts, but the parts are in the wrong order.
Read the ten parts and then put them in the right order. The two pictures are there to help you.

- [ ] a) The two men walk on down the road until they come to a bridge.
- [ ] b) Fred and Bert ask him where he got the fish. He tells them, 'I got it from a river near here.'
- [1] c) Two men, Fred and Bert, are walking along a road.
- [ ] d) Fred says to Bert, 'When you catch a fish, shout and I can pull you up.'
- [ ] e) They meet another man. He's coming in the opposite direction. He's carrying an enormous fish.
- [ ] f) An hour later Bert suddenly shouts, 'Quick, quick. Pull me up! QUICK!'
- [ ] g) 'It's fantastic!! The fish there are jumping so high you can catch them in your hands – from the bridge!'
- [ ] h) 'Have you got a fish?' Fred asks. 'How big is it? Enormous?'
- [ ] i) Then Fred holds Bert's feet while he hangs over the bridge.
- [ ] j) 'No, I haven't got a fish,' Bert answers. 'There's a train coming!!'

6 Now you're here

a Find out what these letters stand for.

Example:
GB = *Great Britain*

1	a.m.	12	VAT
2	ITV	13	RAC
3	DIY	14	p.m.
4	UFO	15	p.t.o.
5	B & B	16	mph
6	BBC	17	LP
7	DJ	18	H & C
8	e.g.	19	AA
9	WC	20	UK
10	MP	21	BR
11	i.e.	22	M & S

b Now make a list of other common abbreviations like these.
Write down what they mean. Ask a British person to help you.

c Compare your lists in class.

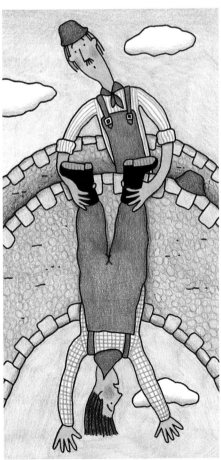

UNIT NINE · LESSON ONE

Where were you?

Dominique wanted to play tennis. Rob and Debbie wanted to play too. So they decided to meet at the tennis courts at three o'clock.

Debbie arrived at three o'clock but Rob and Dominique didn't. She waited for twenty minutes but they still didn't arrive. She was very angry. She phoned home but nobody answered. She then walked home, opened the front door and . . .

Did you have a good game?

No, I didn't—I didn't play.

Because Dominique and Rob didn't arrive. I waited twenty minutes for them. Then I phoned you but you didn't answer. Where were you?

Where were you?

Why didn't you play?

Sorry, we were in the garden.

What do you mean 'Where was I'? Where were *you*?

Oh no, how stupid! We were at the tennis courts in White Rock Gardens.

We were at the tennis courts at three o'clock, but you weren't.

Yes, I was.

Which tennis courts?

The tennis courts in Alexandra Park, of course.

1 Make true sentences

Make true sentences from the table.

Example:
Dominique and Rob were at the tennis courts in White Rock Gardens.

	was	with Rob and Dominique.
		at the tennis courts at 3 o'clock.
Dominique and Rob	wasn't	at the tennis courts in Alexandra Park.
Debbie		at the tennis courts in White Rock Gardens.
Mr and Mrs Bond	were	at home at 3 o'clock.
		in the house at 3 o'clock.
	weren't	in the garden at 3 o'clock.

2 Ask and answer

Ask and answer these questions in pairs.

Example:
A *Did Dominique want to play football?*
B *No, he wanted to play tennis.*

1 Did Rob and Debbie want to go swimming?
2 Did they decide to meet at 2 o'clock?
3 Did Debbie arrive late?
4 Did she wait for half an hour?
5 Did she phone the police?
6 Did her parents answer the phone?
7 Did she walk to the beach?
8 Did Rob and Dominique arrive home before her?

3 Interview Debbie

a Complete the questions with *did, was* or *were*.

b Write Debbie's answers to the questions.

You *What . . . . you want to play?*
Debbie *I . . . .*
You *Who . . . . you want to play with?*
Debbie *. . . .*
You *Where . . . . . you decide to meet?*
Debbie *. . . .*
You *What time . . . . you arrive?*
Debbie *. . . . .*

You *. . . . Dominique and Rob there?*
Debbie *. . . .*
You *How long . . . you wait?*
Debbie *. . . .*
You *What . . . you do then?*
Debbie *. . . .*
You *. . . your mother answer the phone?*
Debbie *. . . . .*
You *. . . . . you angry?*
Debbie *. . . .*
You *. . . . Dominique and Rob at home when you arrived?*
Debbie *. . . . .*
You *Where . . . . . they at 3 o'clock?*
Debbie *. . . . .*

4 What did you do?

Work in pairs. Ask and answer these questions about what you did yesterday.

Example:
play tennis?
A *Did you play tennis yesterday?*
B *Yes I did. / No I didn't.*

1 play football?
2 arrive at school on time?
3 listen to pop music?
4 phone a friend?
5 wait for a bus?
6 walk to school?
7 watch television?
8 answer the phone?

5 Where were you?

Work in groups.

a Student A thinks of where he/she was at a certain time yesterday or last weekend, etc.

b Student A tells the rest of the group the time. They try to guess where he/she was at that time.

Example:
A *Yesterday, at 10 o'clock in the evening.*
B *Were you in bed?*
A *No, I wasn't.*
C *Were you at the cinema?*
A *No, I wasn't.*
D *Were you in the bath?*
A *Yes, you're right. I was.*

c A different student takes over from student A.

Grammar summary: page 84

📺 Making suggestions

Greg *What shall we do this afternoon?*
Sally *Shall we play tennis?*
Greg *No, it's too hot.*
Sally *Why don't we go for a swim?*
Greg *No, the water's too cold.*
Sally *Well, let's sit on the beach then.*
Greg *Yes OK, good idea.*

1 Act it out

Read the dialogue in pairs. Change roles.

2 What are they suggesting?

One student at a time mimes a suggestion. The rest of the class must guess what he/she is suggesting.

Example:
Let's buy an ice-cream.

3 What shall we do?

Work in pairs.

Student A looks at the pictures and makes suggestions. Student B answers.

Example:

A *Shall* | *we play mini-golf?*
Why don't |
Let's play mini-golf.

B *Yes OK, good idea.*
No | *let's* | . . .
| *why don't we* |

1

2

3

4

5

6

4 Making excuses

Now student A makes the same suggestions as in exercise 3, but student B makes an excuse. Choose from:

No, it's too	hot.
	expensive.
	cold.
	late.
	windy.
	wet.

Example:
A *Why don't we play badminton?*
B *No, it's too windy.*

5 Role play

Work in pairs. Student A reads the instructions below. Student B reads the instructions on page 80.

Student A

You want to do something with Student B. Make suggestions.

Example:
Why don't we go for a walk?

You must *continue* making suggestions until Student B agrees with you.

6 Making arrangements

a 🖾 Work in pairs. Practise the dialogue.

David *Let's go to the cinema.*
Paula *Yes OK, good idea.*
David *Which film shall we see?*
Paula *I want to see The Monster from Outer Space.*
David *OK, where shall we meet?*
Paula *Outside the Odeon cinema.*
David *What time shall we meet?*
Paula *At 8 o'clock. The film starts at a quarter past.*

b Look at this film guide from a newspaper. Find out what the following mean:

PG   Sep. progs   U   15   18

WHAT'S ON
FILMS

CANNON CINEMAS 1, 2 & 3: Whiteladies Road, Bristol 733640
1 — Steven Spielberg presents INNER SPACE (PG), in Dolby stereo. Sep. progs. 2.00, 5.00 & 8.00 (Sun. 2.15, 5.00, & 8.00). 2 – Steve Martin ROXANNE (PG). Sep. progs. 2.30, 5.20, & 8.10 (inc. Sun.). 3 – MAURICE (15). Sep. progs. 4.15 & 7.15 (incl. Sun., not Thurs.). Special presentation for one day only Thursday December 3, Sean Connery THE NAME OF THE ROSE (18), 1.30, 4.30 & 7.30. Saturday Late Show at 11 p.m. JAGGED EDGE (15).

CONCORDE CINEMAS, Stapleton Rd, Eastville. 510377 Concorde 1, OUTRAGEOUS FORTUNES (15) 8.00. From Sun. ALAN LADD as SHANE (U). Sun. 5.00 & 7.30. Wk. 8.00, Concorde 2: BLACK WIDOW (15) 8.00 from Sun. BEVERLY HILLS COP II (15) Sun. 5.00 & 7.30 Wk 8.00

GAIETY CINEMA, Wells Road 776224   MADONNA in WHO'S

c Choose a film you want to see. Practise the dialogue again. Use your own ideas instead of the underlined words. Take it in turns to be A and B.

7 What's missing?

🖾 Listen to these three conversations.

a Match the conversations with the pictures.

b Fill in the missing information under the pictures.

1 Meeting place: . . . . .
  Time: . . . . .

2 Meeting place: . . . . .
  Time: . . . . .

3 Meeting place: . . . . .
  Time: . . . . .

Summary of English in situations

- making arrangements
- making suggestions
- making excuses

1 Sound right

a 🖭 Listen to these phrases and sentences.

Wait for me.
It's an egg.
What's the time?
Fish and chips.
At eight o'clock.
It's slow but cheap.
Speak to me.
He's from France.
A cup of tea.

b Listen again. Circle the words or syllables which are said lightly or quickly.

Example:

Wait (for) me.

c Listen and repeat the phrases and sentences.
Notice that these words are usually said very lightly or quickly:

a   an   the
for   at   to   from   of
and   but

2 Listen to this

🖭 Listen to the six voices and write down their jobs.
Choose from the jobs in the box.

teacher	waiter
doctor	photographer
taxi driver	bank clerk
soldier	telephone operator
dentist	farmer
pilot	mechanic
shop assistant	disc jockey
chemist	secretary

1 ....
2 ....
3 ....
4 ....
5 ....
6 ....

3 Work on words

5 (down)   1 (across)   2
1 (down)   3   6   9
5 (across)   4   10   11   7   8

58

4 Play games in English

Think of a word

a Form two teams. On a piece of paper, each team writes these categories:

a country	
a sport	
something you eat	
something you drink	
something you wear	

b The teacher says a letter, for example B. The two teams try to think of words in the five categories which begin with that letter.

a country	Belgium
a sport	basketball
something you eat	banana
something you drink	beer
something you wear	boots

The first team to finish is the winner. The teacher then says another letter.

5 Read and think

a Read this story from a newspaper.

Unhappy ending

Mrs Joyce Harris from Birmingham telephoned the fire brigade when she noticed her house was on fire. Ten minutes later a fire engine arrived. Mrs Harris was outside her house. She was very worried

'My husband and son!' she shouted. 'They're still inside!'

Four firemen rushed into the house. They discovered Mr Harris and his teenage son Wayne in the sitting room. They were in front of the television. The room was full of smoke.

The firemen picked them up and carried them outside. But Mr Harris and his son were not pleased. In fact they were angry.

'Why did you stay in the house when it was on fire?' a fireman asked Mr Harris.

Mr Harris answered, 'We didn't want to leave because we wanted to watch the end of *Dallas*!'

b Are these sentences true or false?

	True	False
1 Mr Harris telephoned the fire brigade.	☐	☐
2 Mrs Harris waited for the fire brigade outside her house.	☐	☐
3 Her husband and son were still inside the house.	☐	☐
4 Mrs Harris discovered her husband and son in the sitting room.	☐	☐
5 The television was on fire.	☐	☐
6 The firemen carried the television outside.	☐	☐
7 Mrs Harris was very angry with the firemen.	☐	☐
8 Mr Harris stayed in the house to watch television.	☐	☐
9 Mr Harris and his son liked *Dallas*.	☐	☐

6 Now you're here

a The following are all common abbreviations. Find out what they mean.

Example:
Sat. = *Saturday*

1	Mon.	9	plc
2	info.	10	hr
3	prog.	11	min.
4	Feb.	12	dept.
5	tel.	13	incl.
6	Bros.	14	in.
7	etc.	15	ft.
8	no.	16	lb.

b Make a list of other abbreviations you see and try to find out what they mean.
Ask a British person if he/she can think of any more.

c Compare your list with other students' lists.

🎞 Dominique's day out

One Saturday morning Dominique went to London. He went by coach with the other students on his course.

They left at 9 o'clock in the morning, and they got to London at 11 o'clock.

First they did some sightseeing and then they had lunch. After that they had the afternoon free.

Dominique had a good time. He took a lot of photos and bought a lot of souvenirs. But at the end of the day . . .

I'm worried about Dominique. Miss Fox rang an hour ago . . .

What's the matter, Sue?

What did she say?

Dominique didn't come back with them. He missed the coach.

Where is he now?

I don't know. I'm very worried.

The telephone rings

Hello . . . 712660.

Is that Mrs Bond?

Dominique! Where are you?

I'm at the station. I came back by train.

How did you miss the coach?

Oh, I met some French students and I forgot the time. Then I got lost . . .

Don't worry, Dominique! I'm coming to get you now. Stay there!

Just a moment, Mrs Bond. There's another problem.

What is it?

I caught the wrong train. I'm not at Hastings station. I'm at Brighton . . .

1 Questions and answers

a Match the questions on the left with the answers on the right.

Example: 1 – i

1 When did they go to London?
2 How did they go?
3 What time did they leave?
4 What time did they get to London?
5 What did they do in London?
6 Did Dominique have a good time?
7 Who did Dominique meet?
8 Why did Dominique miss the coach?
9 How did Dominique come home?
10 Where did the train go to?

a) Yes, he did.
b) Some French students.
c) To Brighton.
d) By coach.
e) At eleven o'clock.
f) By train.
g) They went sightseeing.
h) At nine o'clock.
i) On Saturday.
j) Because he forgot the time.

b Work in pairs. Student A asks the same questions, student B answers them without looking at the answers above. Change roles.

2 What happened when?

a In what order did these things happen in the story?

☐ Dominique got lost.
☐ Miss Fox rang Mrs Bond.
☐ The coach went to London.
☐ Dominique got to Brighton.
☐ Dominique caught the wrong train.
☐ The coach left Hastings.
☐ Dominique forgot the time.
☐ Dominique missed the coach.
☐ Dominique did some sightseeing.

b Retell the whole story.

3 What did you do?

a Work in pairs. Find out what your partner did yesterday evening. Ask him/her questions using the verbs in the box.

| go out | listen | meet | ring |
| read | go to bed | eat | have |

Ask questions like these:
Did you go out?
What did you have for dinner?

b Think of your own questions using other verbs.

c Now find out what he/she did last summer, using these verbs:

| go | stay | spend | buy | do | have |

Ask questions like these:
Did you go abroad?
Where did you stay?
Did you have a good time?

d Tell the rest of the class what your partner did yesterday evening/last summer.

4 Quick questions

Go round the class, asking and answering quick questions like this:
Did you go to the cinema last week?

Find as many students as you can who:

went to the cinema last week
bought some clothes yesterday
had a bath last night
took some photos last weekend
came to school late yesterday
wrote a letter at the weekend.

The 'winner' is the student with the most names after five minutes.

5 Start of the day

a Work in pairs. Student A reads the information about Suzanna below. Student B reads the information about Patrick on page 81.

b Student A asks student B questions about Patrick, and fills in the missing information about him.

Example:
A *What time did he get up this morning?*
B *He got up at half past seven.*

c Student B asks student A the same questions about Suzanna and fills in the missing information about her.

Suzanna

Got up at: *7.30*
Had breakfast at: *8.00*
Had for breakfast: *toast and coffee*
Had a shower: *Yes*
Left home at: *8.40*
Got to school at: *8.55*
Came to school by: *bus*

Patrick

Got up at: . . . . .
Had breakfast at: . . . . .
Had for breakfast: . . . . .
Had a shower: . . . . .
Left home at: . . . . .
Got to school at: . . . . .
Came to school by: . . . . .

Grammar summary: page 85

1 What are they?

Write down the correct names of the clothes.

Shopping

Shop assistant *Can I help you?*
First customer *No, I'm just looking, thanks.*

(pause)

Shop assistant *Can I help you?*
Second customer *Yes, I'm looking for a pair of jeans.*
Shop assistant *What size are you?*
Second customer *I'm size 30, I think.*
Shop assistant *These are all 30 waist.*

(one minute later)

Second customer *Can I try these on, please?*
Shop assistant *Yes, the changing room's over there.*

(a little later)

Second customer *They're too big. Have you got size 28?*
Shop assistant *Yes, here you are.*

(one minute later)

Second customer *Yes, they're OK. How much are they?*
Shop assistant *They're £24.99.*
Second customer *Right, I'll have them, please.*

Measurements

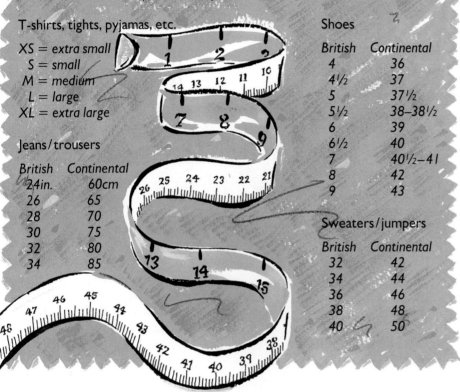

British shops are slowly changing over to the metric system (instead of inches/feet/yards). Many department stores use both systems whereas most small clothes shops still usually use the British measurements.

T-shirts, tights, pyjamas, etc.

XS = extra small
 S = small
M = medium
 L = large
XL = extra large

Jeans/trousers

British	Continental
24 in.	60 cm
26	65
28	70
30	75
32	80
34	85

Shoes

British	Continental
4	36
4½	37
5	37½
5½	38–38½
6	39
6½	40
7	40½–41
8	42
9	43

Sweaters/jumpers

British	Continental
32	42
34	44
36	46
38	48
40	50

2 Act it out

a Practise the dialogue opposite in groups of three. Use your own sizes.

b Work in pairs. Imagine you want to buy other clothes. Act out the dialogue.

3 What's missing?

🖳 Listen to the dialogue, and then fill in the missing information in the table below.

Clothes	Colour	Price	Size
1 ...	...	...	...
2 ...	...	...	...
3 ...	...	...	...

4 Bring me a . . .

a Form two teams. One student from each team stands at the front of the class.

b The teacher then asks these two students to bring certain things from the other people in their teams.

Examples:
a white sock
a black shoe
a red sweater
a brown jacket
a green handbag

The first team to give each object to the teacher gets a point.

5 What's wrong?

What's wrong with these clothes?

Choose from the words in the box.

big	small	long	short

1...   2..
3...   4...

Summary of English in situations
• buying clothes • talking about sizes and colours

1 Sound right

a 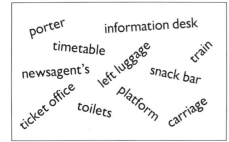 Listen and underline the words or syllables which are said heavily.

Example:
They <u>got</u> to <u>London</u> at el<u>even</u> o'clock.

1 Dominique went to London.
2 He went by coach.
3 He took some photographs.
4 How did you miss the coach?
5 I met some French students, and I forgot the time.
6 I'm coming to get you now.
7 I caught the wrong train.
8 I'm not at Hastings station.

b Now practise saying the sentences. Try to say the 'heavy' words and syllables as heavily as possible, and the others as quickly or lightly as possible.

2 Work on words

At the station

porter   information desk
timetable   left luggage   train
newsagent's   snack bar
ticket office toilets platform carriage

What are the things you can see in the picture? Fill them in below.

1 ....
2 ....
3 ....
4 ....
5 ....
6 ....
7 ....
8 ....
9 ....
10 ....
11 ....

3 Read and think

Who says what?

Read the following and decide which of the people in the picture on page 64 says each of them.

1 ...
> Single or return?

2 ...
> Bye! Have a good journey.

3 ...
> I want to go to Manchester tomorrow. Can you tell me the times of trains?

4 ...
> With or without milk?

5 ...
> Is this the right platform for the London train?

6 ...
> Can I have a ticket to London, please?

7 ...
> See you soon. Don't forget to write!

8 ...
> What time of day do you want to travel?

9 ...
> Can I have a cup of tea, please?

10 ...
> Yes, it is. It'll be in in about five minutes.

4 Listen to this

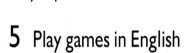 This morning Susan, the maid, took a cup of tea to Lady Bartley ...

Now listen to what happened after that and mark the sentences with a tick (√) or a cross (×).

The Bartleys had dinner at 8.15. ☐
They had steak for dinner. ☐
After dinner they saw a film. ☐
They didn't go out during the evening. ☐
Lady Bartley went to bed half an hour before Lord Bartley. ☐
They slept in the same bedroom. ☐

5 Play games in English

Alibi

The police think Lady Bartley was murdered at about 11 o'clock. They want to interview George (the gardener) and Susan (the maid).

a Two students, George and Susan, go out of the room. They read their instructions on page 81.

b The other students in the class are detectives. They must think of at least twenty questions to ask George and Susan.

George and Susan say:

they left the house at 7 o'clock
they went to London
they had dinner in a restaurant
they went to the cinema
they went to a disco.

Examples of questions the detectives can ask:
What time did you go out last night?
Where did you have dinner?
What was the name of the disco?

c The detectives ask Susan the questions and write down her answers. They then do the same with George.

MURDER AT
BARTLEY TOWERS
A. D. YOUNGER

d If there are three or more differences in their answers, they are guilty – they killed Lady Bartley.

6 Now you're here

Ask a British person these questions. If the answer is 'yes', ask a second question, using the word in brackets. Write down the answers you get.

Example:
A *Did you buy anything yesterday? (What?)*
B *Yes, I did.*
A *What did you buy?*
B *A newspaper and a new pair of shoes.*

- Did you drink any coffee yesterday? (How much?)
- Did you spend any money? (How much?)
- Did you ring anyone? (Who?)
- Did you lose anything? (What?)
- Did you read a newspaper? (Which?)
- Did you get any letters? (Who from?)
- Did you watch television? (What?)
- Did you go to bed late? (What time?)

Tell the rest of the class your most interesting answers.

GRAMMAR IN ACTION

Trivial Pursuit

Sammy It's your turn now, Dominique. Throw the dice.

Dominique Three. 1–2–3. Green.

Debbie OK, boys. Which is longer, a metre or a yard?

Rob That's easy – a yard.

Debbie Wrong!

Sammy Give me the dice. It's our turn . . . Five. 1–2–3–4–5. Blue.

Rob Which is hotter, 100 degrees Celsius or 100 degrees Fahrenheit?

Sammy 100 degrees Celsius is hotter than 100 degrees Fahrenheit.

Rob Brilliant!

Debbie Let me throw now . . . One. Orange.

Dominique Which is more intelligent – a dolphin or a whale?

Debbie Eh . . . that's more difficult . . . er . . . a dolph . . . – no, a whale!

Dominique Wrong!

Rob It's my turn then . . . Four. Yellow.

Sammy Which planet is the nearest to Earth?

Dominique I think it's . . . it's Venus.

Rob Good, Dominique! You're cleverer than I thought!

Debbie But that was much easier than our last question!

Rob Rubbish!

Dominique It's my turn . . . Two. Red.

Debbie What's the most common word in the English language?

Dominique Please!

Rob No! It's–

Sammy Too late. The answer's 'the'.

Rob But I knew it! This is a silly game!

Debbie It's just because you're losing!

1 Who's who?

Who does the following? Tick (√) the right answer.

Choose from: Debbie (A) Sammy (B) Rob (C) Dominique (D).

	A	B	C	D
1 Who plays with Dominique?	☐	☐	☐	☐
2 Who plays with Debbie?	☐	☐	☐	☐
3 Who thinks a yard is longer than a metre?	☐	☐	☐	☐
4 Who knows 100°Centigrade is hotter than 100°Fahrenheit?	☐	☐	☐	☐
5 Who thinks a whale is more intelligent than a dolphin?	☐	☐	☐	☐
6 Who knows Venus is the nearest planet to Earth?	☐	☐	☐	☐
7 Who thinks 'please' is the most common word in English?	☐	☐	☐	☐
8 Who thinks Trivial Pursuit is a silly game?	☐	☐	☐	☐

2 Make comparisons

a Write sentences using the words and information in the pictures.

Example: kilometre (short) mile

A kilometre is shorter than a mile.

1 30°C (hot) 30°F

2 Jupiter (big) Mars

3 kilo (heavy) pound

4 100 mph (fast) 100 kph

b Now write sentences comparing the things in the pictures using the words in the box.

light	slow	cold	small	long

Example:
A mile is longer than a kilometre.

3 Compare them

a Look at the information in the table.

	Sammy	Rob	Dominique	Debbie
Age	16 yrs, 3 mths	15 yrs, 4 mths	16 yrs, 1 mth	16 yrs, 8 mths
Height	1.65 metres	1.72 metres	1.76 metres	1.62 metres
Weight	52 kilos	65 kilos	63 kilos	50 kilos
Shoe size	36	41	43	37

b Work in pairs. Ask and answer questions like this:

A *Who's older, Sammy or Rob?*
B *Sammy's older than Rob.*
A *Who's got bigger feet, Sammy or Debbie?*
B *Debbie's got bigger feet than Sammy.*

Use adjectives like the ones in the box.

old / young	heavy / light
tall / short	big / small

c Now ask and answer questions like this:

A *Who's the oldest?*
B *Debbie is.*
A *Who's got the biggest feet?*
B *Dominique has.*

4 School subjects

a Make a list of the subjects you do at school. They probably include some of the following.

English	chemistry
history	gymnastics
maths	biology
physics	art
geography	religious knowledge

b Compare the subjects on your list, using adjectives like the ones in the box.

easy / difficult	boring
useful	enjoyable
important	interesting

Example:
English is more important than gymnastics.

c Now write sentences like these:

I'm better at English than maths.
I'm worse at chemistry than biology.

d Now write sentences like these:

I think English is the most important school subject.
My best subject is maths.
My worst subject is history.

5 Class survey

a Form groups. Ask each other questions to find out who is:

- the oldest / youngest / tallest / shortest in the group
- the student with the biggest / smallest feet
- the student from the biggest family.

b Now vote on which student in the class is:

- the best at English
- the most hard-working
- the laziest
- the noisiest.

Grammar summary: page 85

Asking permission

Tomas *Is it all right if I come home late this evening?*
Mrs Hall *Yes, all right. Where are you going?*
Tomas *To a party.*
Mrs Hall *What time does it finish?*
Tomas *Oh, about midnight.*
Mrs Hall *All right, but you must be home by half past twelve.*
Tomas *Don't worry, I will.*
Can I have a front door key, please?
Mrs Hall *Yes, of course.*
Tomas *And is it OK if I use your bike?*
Mrs Hall *No, I'm sorry. It hasn't got any lights.*

1 Act it out

a Practise the dialogue above in pairs.

b Now write dialogues for the following situations.
Use these phrases:

Can I . . .?
Is it all right if I . . .?
Yes, of course / Yes, all right.

Example:

A *Is it all right if I close the window?*
B *Yes, of course.*

1

2

3

4

5

c Act out your dialogues in pairs. Change roles.

d Now think of reasons for not giving permission in each of the situations.

Example:
A *Is it all right if I open the window?*
B *No, I'm sorry, I'm cold.*

e In pairs, practise refusing permission.

6

f Think of other situations where you must ask permission.
In pairs, practise asking permission.

Example:
A *Can I borrow your tennis racket?*
B *Yes, of course.*
　　　　or
No, I'm sorry, I'm using it.

2 Dates

a Learn the ordinal numbers (first, second, etc.) and months on page 86.

b Note that you write 21 (st) August, 1988, or 21/8/88, but you say 'the twenty-first of August, nineteen eighty-eight'.

c Write the date of your birthday and the birthdays of other people in your family.

d Form two teams. Ask each other questions like:
What's the third month of the year?
What's the eleventh month of the year?

3 A survey

a Each student writes down on a piece of paper the twelve months of the year.

b Students then go round the class asking: 'When's your birthday?'
They tick (√) the month of the year for each answer and add the date.

Example:
A *When's your birthday?*
B *The third of March.*

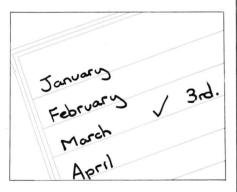

c The teacher then asks:
'Which month is the most 'popular' for birthdays?'
'Which month is the least 'popular' for birthdays?'
'Are there any students in the class with the same birthday?'

4 A quiz

a Form two teams. Students have their books closed. The teacher asks one team at a time:

 1 Which is the shortest month of the year?
 2 Which month has the longest day?
 3 Which month has the shortest day?
 4 In which month is the third letter P?
 5 Which month comes after June?
 6 Which month comes before September?
 7 Which month comes between January and March?
 8 In which month is the last letter L?
 9 Which month has the shortest name?
10 Which month has the longest name?
11 Which month doesn't always have the same number of days?
12 Which three months begin with the same letter?

b Now ask each other similar questions. You have 3 minutes to prepare your questions.

5 The four seasons

a Write two sentences about each season in your country.

Examples:
I go skiing in the winter.
It's hot in the summer.

b Compare your sentences in groups.

6 What's the preposition?

a Look at the phrases below.

on	Monday Tuesday morning 3rd June my birthday
in	the morning the summer July 1989
at	night 10 o'clock Christmas the weekend

b Now complete the following sentences, without looking back at the box.
Choose between *in, on* and *at.*

1 My birthday is . . . 5th August.
2 I go to church . . . Sunday.
3 I get up . . . the morning.
4 I was born . . . 1975.
5 I sleep . . . night.
6 It's usually hot . . . the summer.
7 It often snows . . . January.
8 We sometimes go skiing . . . Christmas.

Summary of English in situations

- asking permission
- giving / refusing permission
- talking about dates

1 Sound right

a Find pairs of words (one from each box) which rhyme.
Example: *what – hot*

WHAT	hate
know	blue
one	tea
caught	HOT
two	good
me	light
great	said
would	laugh
bed	short
write	so
word	sun
half	bird

b Form two teams. Students from each team take it in turns to add to the list of rhyming words on the blackboard.

The team with the longest list is the winner.

c Now practise pronouncing the groups of rhyming words on the blackboard.

2 Listen to this

Listen to the descriptions of six people and fill in the missing information.

The tallest man: . . . . metres.
The tallest woman: . . . . metres.
The heaviest man: . . . . kilos.
The lightest baby: . . . . grams.
The oldest person: . . . . years,
                                . . . . days.
The oldest mother: . . . . years,
                                . . . . days.

3 Work on words

What's the missing word?

Example:
England / English
France / *French*

1   short / long
    near / . . .
2   ½ / half
    ¼ / . . .
3   a telephone / a phone
    a bicycle / . . .
4   weight / kilos
    temperature / . . .
5   he / him
    I / . . .
6   hot / hotter
    easy / . . .
7   to know / knew
    to think / . . .
8   6th / sixth
    2nd / . . .
9   to go / to come
    to stand up / . . .
10 July / Summer
    October / . . .
11 60 seconds / a minute
    60 minutes / . . .
12 August / a month
    winter / . . .
13 a man / men
    a person / . . .
14 Monday / on
    December / . . .
15 a wife / a husband
    a daughter / . . .
16 to take / took
    to go / . . .
17 a plane / an airport
    a train / . . .
18 a taxi / a driver
    a plane / . . .
19 to listen / to
    to wait / . . .
20 7 / a week
    365 / . . .

4 Play games in English

Flump

a One student (Student A) thinks of a verb. The other students in the class try to guess the verb by asking questions like this:

Student B *Can you* **flump**?
Student C *Can everybody* **flump**?
Student D *Are you good at* **flumping**?
Student E *Do you often* **flump**?
Student F *When do you* **flump**?
Student G *Is it easy to* **flump**?
Student H *Are you* **flumping** *now*?
Student I *Did you* **flump** *yesterday*?
Student J *Where did you* **flump**?
Student K *Is the answer 'swim'*?

Student A *Yes I can.*
Student A *No, not everybody.*
Student A *Yes, quite good.*
Student A *Yes, quite often.*
Student A *In the summer.*
Student A *Yes, quite easy.*
Student A *No, I'm not.*
Student A *Yes, I did.*
Student A *In the sea.*
Student A *Yes, it is.*

b Student K then thinks of a different verb.

5 Read and think

a Read the following information carefully.

Kim *Tom* *Ben*
Nick *Meg*

Tom is older than Ben.
Kim is younger than Meg.
Meg is older than Nick.
Nick is younger than Tom.
Ben isn't younger than Kim.
Tom isn't older than Meg.
Nick is younger than Kim.

b Now answer these questions.

1 Who is the oldest?
2 Who is the youngest?
3 Who is the oldest boy?

6 Now you're here

a Ask a British person these questions. Make notes of their answers.

1 Which is the second biggest city in Britain?
2 Which is the oldest university in Britain?
3 Which is the biggest county in Britain?
4 Which is the most common girls' name in Britain?
5 Which is the most popular television programme?
6 Which is the most popular radio programme, Radio 1, 2, 3 or 4?
7 Who is the richest person in Britain?
8 What is the youngest age at which you can marry?
9 What is the most expensive car you can buy in Britain?
10 Which is usually the driest month of the year?
11 Which is usually the wettest month of the year?
12 Which is the most popular newspaper?
13 How wide is the English Channel, at its narrowest point?
14 What is the most common name for a pub?
15 Who is the youngest member of the royal family?

b Tell other students in the class your most interesting answers.

I'm going to miss you!

1 Questions and answers

a Match the questions on the left with the answers on the right.

Example: 1 – d

1 Are they going to eat hamburgers?
2 Is Dominique going to pay?
3 Are his friends going to pay?
4 Is Dominique going to miss his friends?
5 Is Sammy going to cry?
6 Is Sammy going to miss Dominique?

a) Yes, he is.
b) Yes, they are.
c) No, she isn't.
d) No, they aren't.
e) Yes, she is.
f) No, he isn't.

b Work in pairs. Student A asks the same questions. Student B answers without looking in the book. Change roles.

2 What's going to happen?

Describe what's going to happen in each of these pictures.

She's going to answer the phone.

1

2

3

4

5

3 Hastings and Rouen

a Compare Dominique's life in Hastings with his life at home, in Rouen, next week. Use the information in the table below.

In Hastings	In Rouen
with the Bonds	with his parents
instant coffee	real coffee
a bicycle	a moped
on the left	on the right
English	French
tennis	rugby
The Daily Mail	*Le Monde*
ketchup	mayonnaise

Write sentences like this:

In Hastings he lives with the Bonds. Next week, in Rouen, he's going to live with his parents again.

b Now make a list of other differences between life in Britain and in your country. Compare them in the same way.

4 Find out

Ask the person next to you the following questions.

● When are you going to go back to your country?
● Are you going to miss anything about Britain? (What?)
● Are you going to miss anybody? (Who?)
● Are you going to write to anybody in Britain? (Who?)
● Are you going to cry when you leave?
● What's the first thing you're going to do when you get home?
● What's the first thing you're going to eat?
● Are you going to come back to Britain? (When?)

Grammar summary: page 85

Saying goodbye

Mrs Hall *Have you got everything?*
Tomas *Just a minute—passport, ticket, money . . . Yes, I've got everything.*
Mrs Hall *I hope you enjoyed yourself.*
Tomas *Yes, I really did. Thank you very much for everything.*
Mrs Hall *Don't forget to write to us.*
Tomas *Don't worry, I won't.*
Mrs Hall *Have a good journey.*
Tomas *Thanks . . . And thank you again for looking after me so well. Goodbye!*
Mrs Hall *Bye!*

1 Act it out

Practise the dialogue above in pairs. Change roles.

2 Questions and answers

a Match the questions on the left with the responses on the right.

Example: 5 – b

1	Can I try them on, please?	a) Yes, that's all, thanks.
2	Can I speak to Mario, please?	b) It's £2.99.
3	Would you like a drink?	c) Nothing.
4	Is it OK if I have a bath?	d) Cheerio.
5	How much is it?	e) Yes, there's a changing room over there.
6	Who's speaking?	f) Yes, here you are.
7	What's the matter?	g) No, I'm sorry, there's no hot water.
8	When's your birthday?	h) That's a pity.
9	Is that everything?	i) No, I'm sorry, he's not in.
10	Bye! See you tomorrow.	j) On 11th August.
11	Can you pass the salt, please?	k) This is Laura.
12	I can't come to the party, I'm afraid.	l) Yes, please.

b Work in pairs. Student A says the sentences on the left. Student B responds without looking at the answers on the right.

3 A quiz

a What do you say if:

1 somebody asks you if you want an ice cream?
2 you want to dance with somebody?
3 you want to know what something costs?
4 somebody needs help?
5 you want to try on a pair of jeans?
6 you want to know the date?
7 you want to know the time?
8 you want to use the telephone?
9 somebody asks if he / she can smoke in your room?
10 you want to buy a cup of coffee?
11 you want to speak to Chris on the phone?
12 you answer the phone and somebody asks for you?

b Look at the pictures and fill in the speech bubbles.

1

2

3

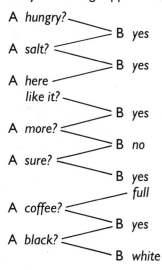

4

4 What do they say?

In this dialogue, A is Mrs Baker, B is a foreign student staying with her. They are having supper.

A *hungry?* — B *yes*

A *salt?* — B *yes*

A *here like it?* — B *yes*

A *more?* — B *no*

A *sure?* — B *yes full*

A *coffee?* — B *yes*

A *black?* — B *white*

a The conversation is written in the shortest possible way. Write it out in full.

b Practise the *polite* version of the dialogue in pairs.

5 Where are they?

Listen to these short conversations.
Write the number of the conversation in the box under the correct picture.

☐

☐

☐

☐

☐

☐

1 London picture quiz

a Divide the class into two or more teams.

b Each team should match the name of each building/place with the correct photograph. Choose names from the box below.

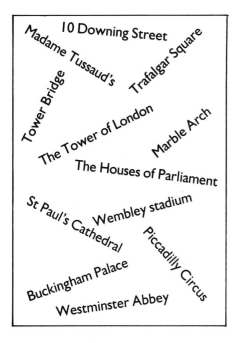

> 10 Downing Street
> Madame Tussaud's
> Trafalgar Square
> Tower Bridge
> The Tower of London
> Marble Arch
> The Houses of Parliament
> St Paul's Cathedral
> Wembley stadium
> Piccadilly Circus
> Buckingham Palace
> Westminster Abbey

c They should then match the photographs with the correct descriptions below.

d A correct name gets one point. A correct sentence gets another point.

A This is where the Prime Minister lives.
B Here you can see wax models of famous people.
C This is the Queen's residence in London.
D MPs debate and argue here, and there is a clock tower with a famous bell in it.

E This building was rebuilt by Christopher Wren after the Great Fire of London, 1666. It has a famous 'whispering gallery'.
F English kings and queens are usually married here. Many of them are also buried here, as well as many famous writers.

G This place has a memorial to Admiral Nelson, and is also famous for its many pigeons.
H This round place is often called the centre of London. There is a statue of Eros in the middle of it.
I It is quite near the City of London. It opens to let ships through.

2 UK quiz

a Divide the class into two teams, A and B.

b Team A answer question 1, team B question 2, etc. If one team can't answer a question, the other team tries to answer it.

Questions

1 What does 'lb' mean?

2 68° Fahrenheit is
  a) 15°
  b) 20°
  c) 25° Celsius.

3 Is a mile about
  a) 1,000
  b) 1,600
  c) 2,000 metres?

4 What does 'mph' mean?

5 Is the capital of Eire
  a) Belfast
  b) Edinburgh
  c) Dublin?

6 What is Wembley famous for?

7 What are these?
  a) *The Guardian*
  b) *The News of the World*
  c) *The Independent*

8 What are these?
  a) Harrods
  b) Selfridges
  c) Marks & Spencer

9 Which of these cities is in Wales?
  a) Cardiff
  b) Bristol
  c) York

10 What does 'L' on a car or motorbike mean?

11 What number do you dial if you want the police?

12 Channels 1 and 2 on British television are BBC. What is Channel 3?

13 You must go to school in Britain
  a) from the age of 5 until you are 16
  b) from the age of 6 until you are 17
  c) from the age of 7 until you are 18.

14 What is the population of Britain?
  a) 35 million
  b) 45 million
  c) 55 million

15 When can you vote in Britain?
  a) When you are 18.
  b) When you are 20.
  c) When you are 21.

16 What is the name of the largest political party in Britain?

17 How old must you be to buy an alcoholic drink in a pub?
  a) 16
  b) 18
  c) 20

18 Is the Princess of Wales married to
  a) Prince Andrew
  b) Prince Philip
  c) Prince Charles?

19 Which of these cities is in Scotland?
  a) Manchester
  b) Glasgow
  c) Southampton

20 What are these?
  a) Vauxhall
  b) Rover
  c) Jaguar

21 'Ulster' is another name for
  a) Scotland
  b) Northern Ireland
  c) the Republic of Ireland.

22 What are these?
  a) Arsenal
  b) Tottenham Hotspur
  c) Queens Park Rangers

23 What are these?
  a) Gatwick
  b) Heathrow
  c) Stanstead

24 What are these?
  a) Kent
  b) Surrey
  c) Hampshire

25 Where is the Loch Ness Monster supposed to live?
  a) England
  b) Scotland
  c) Wales

26 What sort of programmes can you hear on BBC1 Radio 1?
  a) classical music
  b) news and talks
  c) pop music

PAIRWORK: STUDENT B

This material is for use by student B in the information gap exercises earlier in the book.

Unit 2 Lesson 2 Exercise 2 (page 14)

Picture B

Work in pairs. Student A looks at picture A on page 14. Student B looks at picture B above. Try to find the six differences between the two pictures. Ask questions like: *Where are the clothes?*

Unit 2 Lesson 2 Exercise 5 (page 15)

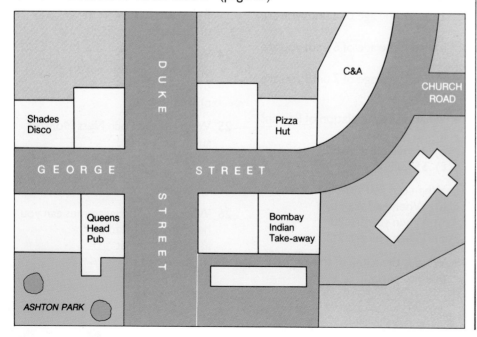

Look at the map.

You want to know where these places are:

1 Barclays Bank
2 the post office
3 the Cannon cinema
4 Boots the Chemist
5 the bus station
6 St Peter's Church

Take it in turns to ask and answer. A starts.

Unit 4 Lesson 1 Exercise 4 (Page 25)

a Work in pairs. Student A looks at the information about Paul on page 25. Student B looks at the information about Carmen below.

b Student A asks questions about Carmen like this:

A *Does she like English pop music?*
B *Yes, she does.*

c Student B asks questions about what Paul likes or doesn't like.

Paul

English pop music: . . .	
English food: . . .	
Spanish food: . . .	
English weather: . . .	

Carmen

English pop music:	YES
English food:	NO
Spanish food:	YES
English weather:	NO

Unit 4 Lesson 2 Exercise 4
(Page 26)

Work in pairs. Student A looks at the list of programmes on Radio 1 on page 26.

Student B looks at the list of programmes below.

Ask each other questions, and fill in the missing information on your page.

Example:
What time does Simon Mayo start?

TUESDAY

1
| MW 1053 + |
| 1089 kHz |
| 285 + 275 m |
| VHF/FM |
| 88·90·2 |

VHF/FM Stereo between 10.0pm and 12 midnight
News on the half hour from 6.30am until 8.30pm, then 10.0 and 12 midnight

5.30am Adrian John

☐ **Simon Mayo**
with the **Breakfast Show**. Just before **8.0**, an exclusive preview of the new Top 40.

9.30 Simon Bates

11.0 ☐

Edinburgh

with **Mike Read** at Portobello Beach, Edinburgh

12.30pm Newsbeat
with **Frank Partridge**

☐ **Gary Davies**
with this week's Top 40

3.0 Bruno Brookes

5.30 ☐
with **Frank Partridge**

5.45 Peter Powell
At **6.30** Peter reviews the new Top 40 singles.

☐ **Robbie Vincent**
with special guests

10.0-12.0 John Peel

Unit 5 Lesson 2 Exercise 8 (Page 33)

Examples:
B *How much do the shoes cost?*
A *They cost £35.99.*
   How much does the jacket cost?
B *It costs £49.50.*

Unit 7 Lesson 2 Exercise 3 (Page 44)

```
881008     Bond J.R, 1 Surre...                        Tun Wells  30/43   Bone C
210633     Bond Kay, 18 Robertson Ho,Hastings ...      Tun Wells  22485   Bone C
362786     Bond K, 42 Priory Rd                        Tun Wells  28750   Bone C
712718     Bond K.L, 19 Cavendish Dv ...                                  Bone C
354564     Bond L.A, South Riding,Upper Cumberland Wlk ...                Bone C
ge   673   Bond L.R, Leighton,Dower Ho Cres,Southborough ... Hastings 435597  Bone C
s 217591   Bond L.T,                                       Brede  882703   Bone C
lls 42819           20 Gresham Wy,Filsham Pk,St. Leonards-o-s. Hastings 437315  Bone
field 3626  Bond M, Sunnyside,Cackle St ...                                Bone
s 212151   Bond M, 2 Quarry Cres                        Tun Wells  33214   Bone
tford 2789  Bond M.A, 7 Holly Clo,Hailsham Rd...         Burwash   883236   Bone
rden 2592  Bond N.C, 4 Earls Rd                         Tun Wells  43297   Bone
nbury 2260  Bond Norman F.G, Linden,Swiffe La,Broad Oak ...  Forest Rw  3308   Bone
           Bond N.H, 13 Kendal Pk ...             South Godstone 893168   Bor
ngs 422744  Bond N.J, Belnor,Chapel La.                   Smallfield  2443   Bor
ngs 754384  Bond P.D, 2 The Grange                          Otford  4616   Bor
e Gn 830338  Bond P.E.T, 8 Grange Wy ...                                   Bor
ngs 441497  Bond P.F, 21a East Hill Fm,Kemsing ...        Burwash  882294   Bo
ngs 429843  Bond R.A, Unit 14 Waldron Ct Mutton Hall Hill ... Hastings 429077  Bo
ersham  380  Bond R.A, Roseneath,Shrub Rd ...            Copthorne 714586   Bo
gh Gn 884491  Bond R.C, 166 Sedlescombe Rd Nth,St. Leonards-o-S.  Fairseat 822889  Bo
mans Pk  403  Bond R.G, 8 Woodland Clo,Crawley Dwn ...     Hastings 422952   Bo
n Wells 34592  Bond R.H.C, Five Acres,Oakfarm La            Sevenoaks 452818   Bo
astings 712533  Bond R.M, 73 Edmund Rd
Hastings 52668  Bond Robert W, Ashgrove Cott,Gracious La ...  Westerham  62567
.Oxted 716714  Bond S, 20 Rodney Av                        Edenbridge 862780
n Wells 510196  Bond S.A, 57 Quebec Av                       Hastings 712660
lastings 753684  Bond S.E, 16 Sunnyside                       Fairseat 823642
tchingham  451  Bond S.G, 7/39 Cornwallis Gdns ...         W Malling 848105
Crowboro 4996  Bond S.W, 45 Timberbank,Meopham,Gravesend ... Hastings 751267
tchingham  430  Bond T, 11 Auden Rd,Larkfield               Tun Wells  41129
.Oxted 712201  Bond T, 15 The Dene
Hastings 813587  Bond T, 6 Vale Rd,Southborough ...          Hastings 754080
.Oxted 717562  Bond T.C, 2 Warren Cotts,Stonelands,W Hoathly ... E Grinstead 28632
Hawkhurst 2564  Bond T.J, 8 Geary Pl,Westfield
taplehurst 892438  Bond T.P, 51 Forest View Rd ...          Bexhill-o-s  224220
evenoaks 458060  Bond V.C, 7 Reedswood Rd,St.Leonards-o-s...   Tenterden  2658
Uckfield 2569  Bond V.F, 1 New Brassey Ct,6,Brassey Rd ...     Uckfield  3219
Buxted 3492  Bond W, 17 Heather Dv,St. Michaels
Crowboro 64110  Bond W.F, 16 Keld Dv                       Bexhill-o-s  218410
E Grinstead 28890  Bond W.G, Pound Ho,Willsley Pound          Rotherfield  244
E Grinstead 314599  Bond William.J, 180 Ninfield Rd
Tonbridge 356862  Bond W.W, Loft Cott 4 New Rd              Paddock Wd  346
Rye 225222  Bondelivery Service Ltd –
Crowboro 2815    29 Eldon Wy                               Horam Rd  22
Sandhurst  518  Bonding Systems Ltd,Adhesives Mfrs,        Paddock Wd  34
Cooden 4453             Vines Cross Rd,Horam               Tonbridge 3567
Biddenden 291813  Bond's Delivery Service, 29 Eldon Wy      Tonbridge 3627
Hastings 751739  Bonds E, 14 Lodge Rd                      Tonbridge 351
           Bonds G, 29 College Av                            Oxted 717
Borough Gn 882470  Bonds R.J, 81 Higham La ...             Sevenoaks 463
Smallfield 2907  Bone A.N.G, 103 Home Pk,Hurst Gn            Groombdge
           Bone B.J, 14 Hurst Fm Road,Weald                  Newick
E Grinstead 25091  Bone C.A, Hamsell Manor Barn,Eridge      Frittenden 85
           Bone C.A, Fir Tree Cott,Station Rd              Hadlow 85
                  ...M Parsonage Fm                        Tonbridge 39
```

Work in pairs. Student A looks at the page from the Hastings telephone directory on page 44. He/She then asks student B for the missing information.

Student B looks at the page from the Hastings telephone directory above and asks student A for the missing information.

Example:
B *What's V.C. Bond's telephone number?*
A *Hastings 712242.*

Unit 7 Lesson 2 Exercise 8 (Page 45)

Student A is going to ask you some questions. Use the information below in your answers. Use complete sentences when you answer.

Tiffany's
8.30
number 91
bus station
next to the Town Hall / opposite the Odeon cinema

Unit 8 Lesson 2 Exercise 5 (Page 51)

Situation 1
Student A phones you to invite you to go out. You don't want to go out with him/her. Make excuses, but be friendly.

Situation 2
You phone student A and invite him/her to play tennis with you. You say where (the place) and when (the time). You've got two tennis rackets, but you haven't got any balls.

Unit 9 Lesson 2 Exercise 5 (Page 57)

The *only* thing you want to do tonight is watch television. *Don't* tell student A this, but make excuses when he/she suggests doing something.

Examples:
No, I'm too tired.
I've got a headache.

Unit 10 Lesson 1 Exercise 5
(Page 61)

a Work in pairs. Student A reads the information about Suzanna on page 61. Student B reads the information about Patrick below.

b Student A asks student B questions about Patrick, and fills in the missing information about him.

Example:
A *What time did he get up this morning?*
B *He got up at half past seven.*

c Student B asks student A the same questions about Suzanna and fills in the missing information about her.

Patrick

Got up at: 7.30
Had breakfast at: *8.20*
Had for breakfast: *cornflakes and tea*
Had a shower: *No*
Left home at: *8.45*
Got to school at: *9.00*
Came to school by: *car*

Suzanna

Got up at: . . . . .
Had breakfast at: . . . . .
Had for breakfast: . . . . .
Had a shower: . . . . .
Left home at: . . . . .
Got to school at: . . . . .
Came to school by: . . . . .

Unit 10 Lesson 3 Exercise 5
(Page 65)

Instructions for Susan and George

The police think that you two murdered Lady Bartley last night at about 11.00.

You say that both of you:

- went to London at 7 o'clock, by taxi.
- came back at 12 o'clock, by taxi.
- had dinner in a restaurant.
- saw a film.
- went to a disco.

Prepare your story of what you did last night. The police will ask you questions, one at a time. You must try to tell *exactly* the same story.

Example questions:
What time did you go out?
How did you go to London?
What time did you have dinner?
Where did you have dinner?
Which film did you see?

If there are three or more differences in the stories you tell the police, then *you* killed Lady Bartley!

Unit 1

to be **(present tense)**

Affirmative	
I am	(I'm)
you are	(you're)
he is	(he's)
she is	(she's)
it is	(it's)
we are	(we're)
you are	(you're)
they are	(they're)

Negative	
I am not	I'm not
you are not	you aren't / you're not
he is not	he isn't / he's not
she is not	she isn't / she's not
it is not	it isn't / it's not
we are not	we aren't / we're not
you are not	you aren't / you're not
they are not	they aren't / they're not

Questions
Am I . . . ?
Are you . . . ?
Is he . . . ?
Is she . . . ?
Is it . . . ?
Are we . . . ?
Are you . . . ?
Are they . . . ?

Possessive adjectives

Personal pronoun	Possessive adjective
I	my
you	your
he	his
she	her
it	its
we	our
you	your
they	their

Apostrophe 's' genitive

When you talk about something which a person has or owns, put 's (an apostrophe + s) after the noun.

Example:
Dominique's bags.
A girl's name.

Unit 2

Demonstratives

this (singular)
these (plural) } here / near you

that (singular)
those (plural) } there / not near you

Plurals of nouns

Nouns usually add − s in the plural.

Examples:
a bedroom − two bedrooms
a bag − three bags

The definite article

The definite article in English is always *the*.
It is the same with all nouns, singular or plural, masculine or feminine.

Examples:
the boy − the boys
the girl − the girls
the room − the rooms

Unit 3

to have got **(present tense)**

Affirmative			
I	have (I've)		got . . .
you	have (you've)		got . . .
he	has	(he's)	got . . .
she	has	(she's)	got . . .
it	has	(it's)	got . . .
we	have (we've)		got . . .
you	have (you've)		got . . .
they	have (they've)		got . . .

Negative
I haven't got . . .
you haven't got . . .
he hasn't got . . .
she hasn't got . . .
it hasn't got . . .
we haven't got . . .
you haven't got . . .
they haven't got . . .

Questions
Have I got . . . ?
Have you got . . . ?
Has he got . . . ?
Has she got . . . ?
Has it got . . . ?
Have we got . . . ?
Have you got . . . ?
Have they got . . . ?

Short answers
Yes, I have. / No, I haven't.
Yes, you have. / No, you haven't.
Yes, he has. / No, he hasn't.
Yes, she has. / No, she hasn't.
Yes, it has. / No, it hasn't.
Yes, we have. / No, we haven't.
Yes, you have. / No, you haven't.
Yes, they have. / No, they haven't.

Indefinite articles

a   before words starting with a consonant (b, c, d, etc), or a consonant sound.

Examples:
a bike
a university

an   before words starting with a vowel sound (a, e, i, o, u)

Examples:
an Amstrad
an old bike

Adjective + noun

Adjectives usually go before the noun.

Example:
a French girl
a terrible temper

Adjectives do not change. They are the same with masculine and feminine nouns, both in the singular and plural.

Example:
an English girl – two English boys

Unit 4

The present simple tense

Affirmative		
I	like	
You	like	
He	likes	coffee.
She	likes	
It	likes	
We	like	
You	like	
They	like	

Negative		
I	do not (don't)	
You	do not (don't)	
He	does not (doesn't)	like coffee.
She	does not (doesn't)	
It	does not (doesn't)	
We	do not (don't)	
You	do not (don't)	
They	do not (don't)	

Questions		
Do	I	
Do	you	
Does	he	
Does	she	like coffee?
Does	it	
Do	we	
Do	you	
Do	they	

Short answers
Yes, I do. / No, I don't.
Yes, you do. / No, you don't.
Yes, he does. / No, he doesn't.
Yes, she does. / No, she doesn't.
Yes, it does. / No, it doesn't.
Yes, we do. / No, we don't.
Yes, you do. / No, you don't.
Yes, they do. / No, they don't.

Unit 5

Adverbs of frequency

- Adverbs of frequency tell you how often a person does something or how often something happens.

- The most common adverbs of frequency are:

  always   usually   often   sometimes hardly ever   never.

- Adverbs of frequency usually go before the main verb.

  Example:
  She always asks too many questions.

- Adverbs of frequency usually go after the verb *to be* (*am, are, is,* etc.) and auxiliary verbs (*can, will, must,* etc.)

  Example:
  He is always right.

Unit 6

can (present tense)

Affirmative		
I	can	
You	can	
He	can	
She	can	speak English.
It	can	
We	can	
You	can	
They	can	

Negative		
I	can't	
You	can't	
He	can't	
She	can't	speak English.
It	can't	
We	can't	
You	can't	
They	can't	

Questions	
Can I	
Can you	
Can he	
Can she	speak English?
Can it	
Can we	
Can you	
Can they	

Short answers
Yes, I can./No, I can't. Yes, you can./No, you can't. Yes, he can./No, he can't. Yes, she can./No, she can't. Yes, it can./No, it can't. Yes, we can./No, we can't. Yes, you can./No, you can't. Yes, they can./No, they can't.

Unit 7

Present continuous (progressive) tense

Use the present continuous when you talk about what is happening now, at this moment.

Example:
I'm peeling the potatoes.

Affirmative	
I'm You're He's She's It's We're You're They're	working.

Negative		
I'm	not	
You	aren't/	You're not
He	isn't/	He's not
She	isn't/	She's not
It	isn't/	It's not
We	aren't/	We're not
You	aren't/	You're not
They	aren't/	They're not

(working.)

Questions	
Am I Are you Is he Is she Is it Are we Are you Are they	working?

Short answers
Yes, I am./No, I'm not. Yes, you are./No, you aren't. Yes, he is./No, he isn't. Yes, she is./No, she isn't. Yes, it is./No, it isn't. Yes, we are./No, we aren't. Yes, you are./No, you aren't. Yes, they are./No, they aren't.

Unit 8

some/any

- Positive sentences: *some*

  Example:
  I want some Coca-Cola.

- Negative sentences: *any*

  Example:
  We haven't got any Coca-Cola.

- Questions: *any*

  Example:
  Have you got any Pepsi Cola?

Singular	Plural
There is/isn't Is there . . . ?	There are/aren't Are there . . . ?

Unit 9

Past simple tense: regular verbs

Affirmative	
I You He She It We You They	arrived yesterday.

Negative	
I You He She It We You They	didn't arrive yesterday.

Questions		
Did	I you he she it we you they	arrive yesterday?

Short answers
Yes, I did./No, I didn't. Yes, you did./No, you didn't. Yes, he did./No, he didn't. Yes, she did./No, she didn't. Yes, it did./No, it didn't. Yes, we did./No, we didn't. Yes, you did./No, you didn't. Yes, they did./No, they didn't.

Past simple tense: to be

Affirmative	
I	was
You	were
He	was
She	was
It	was
We	were
You	were
They	were

Negative		
I	was not	(wasn't)
You	were not	(weren't)
He	was not	(wasn't)
She	was not	(wasn't)
It	was not	(wasn't)
We	were not	(weren't)
You	were not	(weren't)
They	were not	(weren't)

Questions
Was I . . . ?
Were you . . . ?
Was he . . . ?
Was she . . . ?
Was it . . . ?
Were we . . . ?
Were you . . . ?
Were they . . . ?

Unit 10

Past simple: irregular verbs

Affirmative
He went to London.

Negative
He didn't go to London.

Questions
Did he go to London?

Present / Infinitive	Past
go	went
leave	left
get	got
do	did
have	had
take	took
buy	bought
ring	rang
say	said
come	came
meet	met
forget	forgot
catch	caught

Unit 11

Comparatives of adjectives

- Add the ending – *er* to short adjectives.

  Example:
  A metre is longer than a yard.

- Put the word *more* before long adjectives.

  Example:
  A dolphin is more intelligent than a whale.

Superlatives of adjectives

- Add the ending – *est* to short adjectives.

  Example:
  Venus is the nearest planet to Earth.

- Put the word *most* before long adjectives.

  Example:
  What is the most common word in English?

  NB Put *the* before the superlatives.

Irregular comparatives/ superlatives

	comparative	superlative
good bad	better worse	the best the worst

Unit 12

Future tense: going to

Affirmative	
I'm You're He's She's It's We're You're They're	going to leave.

Negative	
I'm not You aren't / You're not He isn't / He's not She isn't / She's not It isn't / It's not We aren't / We're not You aren't / You're not They aren't / They're not	going to leave.

Questions	
Am I Are you Is he Is she Is it Are we Are you Are they	going to leave?

Short answers	
Yes, I am.	No, I'm not.
Yes, you are.	No, you aren't. / You're not.
Yes, he is.	No, he isn't. / No, he's not.
Yes, she is.	No, she isn't. / No, she's not.
Yes, it is.	No, it isn't. / No, it's not.
Yes, we are.	No, we aren't. / No, we're not.
Yes, you are.	No, you aren't. / No, you're not.
Yes, they are.	No, they aren't. / No, they're not.

Days of the week

Sunday
Monday
Tuesday
Wednesday
Thursday
Friday
Saturday

Months of the year

January
February
March
April
May
June
July
August
September
October
November
December

Seasons

Spring
Summer
Autumn
Winter

Numbers

Cardinal		Ordinal	
1	one	1st	first
2	two	2nd	second
3	three	3rd	third
4	four	4th	fourth
5	five	5th	fifth
6	six	6th	sixth
7	seven	7th	seventh
8	eight	8th	eighth
9	nine	9th	ninth
10	ten	10th	tenth
11	eleven	11th	eleventh
12	twelve	12th	twelfth
13	thirteen	13th	thirteenth
14	fourteen	14th	fourteenth
15	fifteen	15th	fifteenth
16	sixteen	16th	sixteenth
17	seventeen	17th	seventeenth
18	eighteen	18th	eighteenth
19	nineteen	19th	nineteenth
20	twenty	20th	twentieth
21	twenty-one	21st	twenty-first
22	twenty-two	22nd	twenty-second
23	twenty-three	23rd	twenty-third
24	twenty-four	24th	twenty-fourth
25	twenty-five	25th	twenty-fifth
26	twenty-six	26th	twenty-sixth
27	twenty-seven	27th	twenty-seventh
28	twenty-eight	28th	twenty-eighth
29	twenty-nine	29th	twenty-ninth
30	thirty	30th	thirtieth
31	thirty-one	31st	thirty-first
40	forty	40th	fortieth
50	fifty	50th	fiftieth
60	sixty	60th	sixtieth
70	seventy	70th	seventieth
80	eighty	80th	eightieth
90	ninety	90th	ninetieth
100	one / a hundred	100th	one / a hundredth
101	one / a hundred and one	101st	one / a hundred and first

This list contains the new, active vocabulary introduced in each unit. The words are listed in the order in which they appear in the text.

Unit 1
Lesson 1

first
meeting
French
language course
husband
rude
bag
over there
heavy

Unit 2
Lesson 1

bathroom
loo
bedroom
quite
wardrobe
drawer
clothes
flower
doll

Unit 2
Lesson 2

mess
floor
excuse me
post office
opposite
cinema
between
chemist's
you're welcome

Unit 3
Lesson 1

hi
news
how about . . . ?
at the moment
what's . . . like?
terrible
lucky
computer
a few
game
moped
cc
bike

Unit 3
Lesson 2

spell
full
address
sorry?
postcode

Unit 4
Lesson 1

record
mean (v.)
anything
kind (n.)
singer
word
of course
want (v.)
hear

Unit 4
Lesson 2

turn on
what's the matter?
listen to
pardon?
week
charts (n.)
I'm sorry
understand
hopeless
explain
quick

Unit 5
Lesson 1

parents
ask
many
question (n.)
know
everything
about
live
work
holiday
and so on
embarrassing
habit
sing
bath (n.)

voice
remember
really
sometimes
wear
jeans
tight
forget
nearly
come round
talk about
instead
dance (v.)

Unit 5
Lesson 2

cash (v.)
traveller's cheque
passport
here you are
sign (v.)
fill in
date (n.)
money

Unit 6
Lesson 1

accent
guess (v.)
Spain
Italy
wrong
again
what a pity
speak
a bit of
worry (v.)
come on
let's
swim (v., n.)

Unit 6
Lesson 2

rule (n.)
late

meal
smoke (v.)
use (v.)
without
permission
play (v.)
loud

Unit 7
Lesson 1

lay the table
peel (v.)
potato
upstairs
probably
as usual
shower (n.)
help (v.)
busy
write
letter
kind (a.)
starve

Unit 7
Lesson 2

double
zero
message
ring (v.)

Unit 8
Lesson 1

beach
barbecue
evening
hamburger
only
sausage
left (a.)
I'm afraid
mustard
ketchup
different

Unit 8
Lesson 2

would you like
to . . . ?

Unit 9
Lesson 1

too
decide
meet
court
arrive
wait for
still
angry
phone (v.)
nobody
answer (v.)
then
walk (v.)
open (v.)
front door
garden
stupid

Unit 9
Lesson 2

afternoon
hot
cold
water
sit
idea

Unit 10
Lesson 1

morning
go (went)
by coach
with
leave (left)

get to (got to)
sightseeing
lunch
free
take (took)
photo
buy (bought)
end
ring (rang)
hour
ago
say
miss (v.)
train
station
meet (met)
forget (forgot)
get lost
stay (v)
another
catch (caught)

Unit 10
Lesson 2

look for
a pair of
size
think
waist
later
try on
changing room

Unit 11
Lesson 1

Trivial Pursuit
turn (n.)
throw
dice
green
long
yard
easy
give
blue
degree
Celsius
Fahrenheit
brilliant
orange
intelligent
dolphin
whale
difficult
yellow

planet
earth
clever
think (thought)
last (a.)
rubbish
red
common
know (knew)
silly
because
lose

Unit 11
Lesson 2

party
finish (v.)
key
light (n.)

Unit 12
Lesson 1

miss (v.)
pay (v.)
food
write
careful
cry (v.)
sure

Unit 12
Lesson 2

ticket
enjoy
journey
look after
well

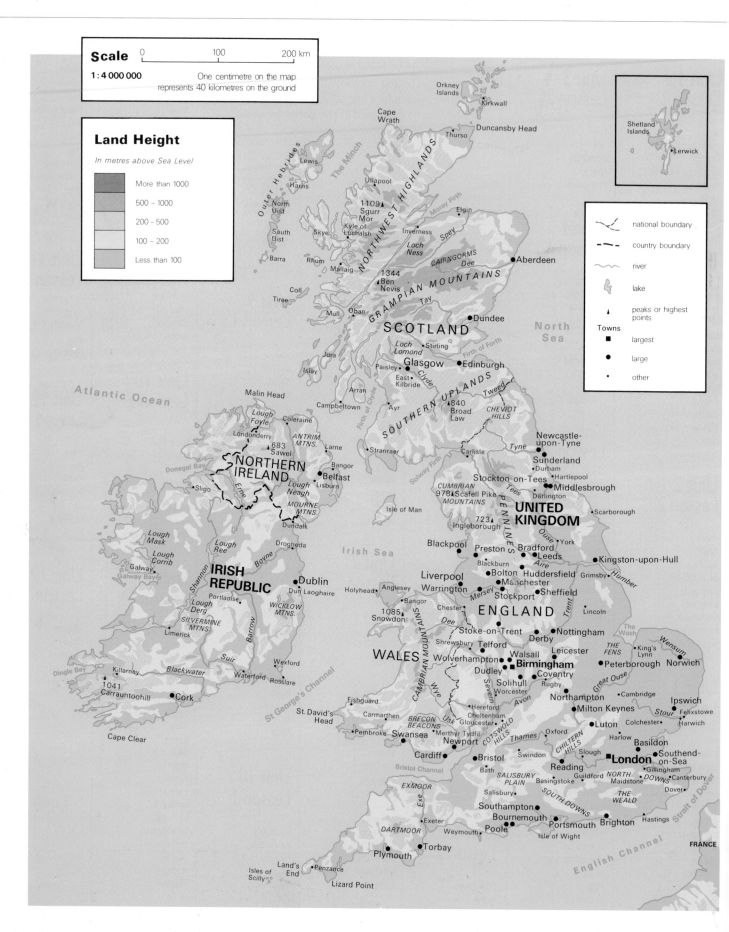

Scale

0   100   200 km

1 : 4 000 000

One centimetre on the map
represents 40 kilometres on the ground

Land Height

In metres above Sea Level

More than 1000

500 – 1000

200 – 500

100 – 200

Less than 100

national boundary

country boundary

river

lake

peaks or highest points

Towns

largest

large

other